I am grateful to God for everything. C.R., you give my life meaning. Love you!

Adilson Silva

2023

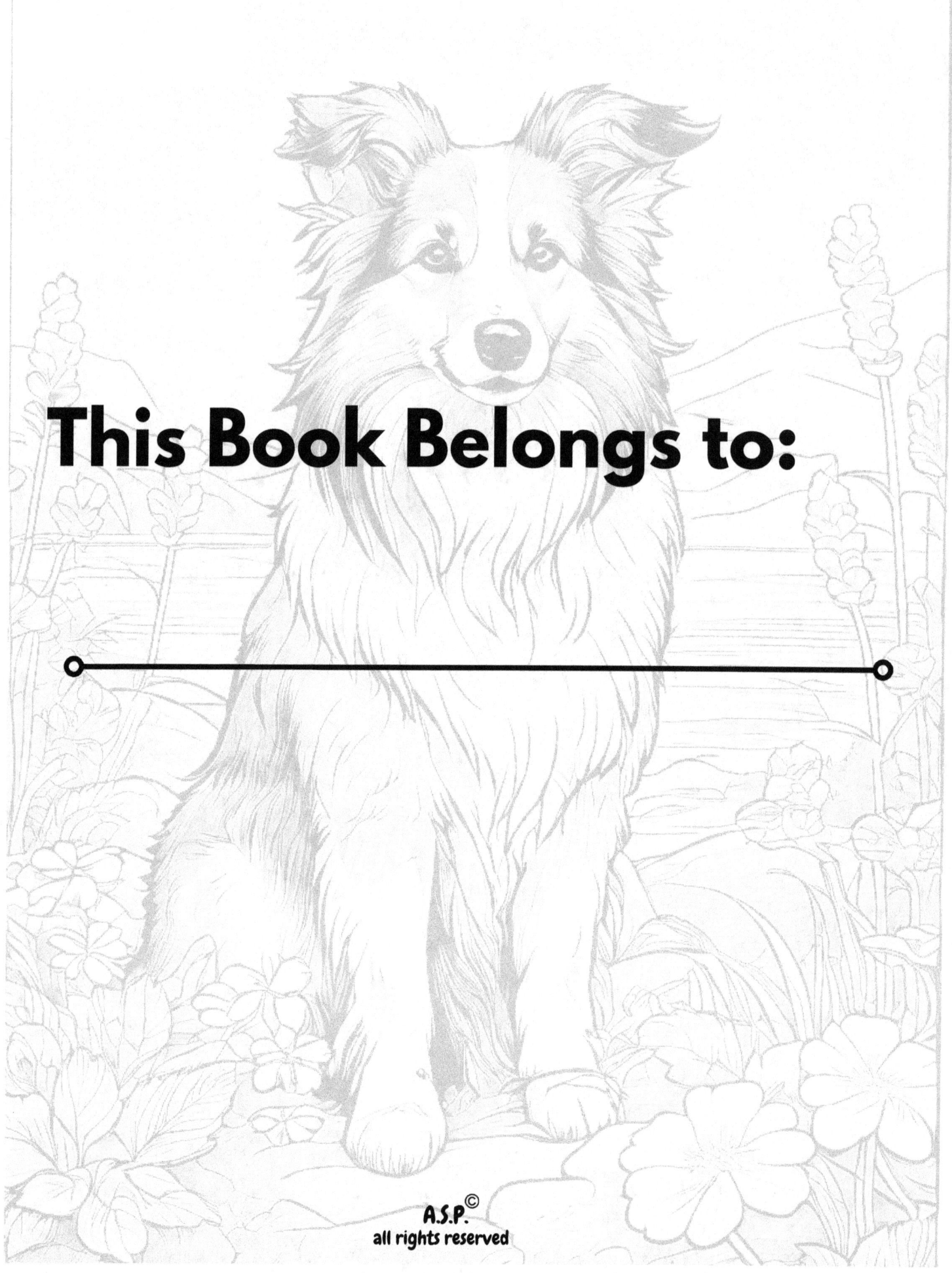
This Book Belongs to:

ALL RIGHTS RESERVED©
2024

No part of this publication may be reproduced, distributed, or transmitted in any form or by any means, including photocopying, recording, or other electronic or mechanical methods, without the prior written permission of the publisher, except for brief quotations incorporated in critical reviews and other specific noncommercial uses. Any unauthorized replica of this work is prohibited.

A.S.P.©
Adilson Silva's publications

Test Color Page

Alaskan Klee Kai: A miniature version of the Alaskan Husky, with striking eyes and a thick coat. Origin: United States. Weight: 4.3-10 kg. Lifespan: 12-16 years.

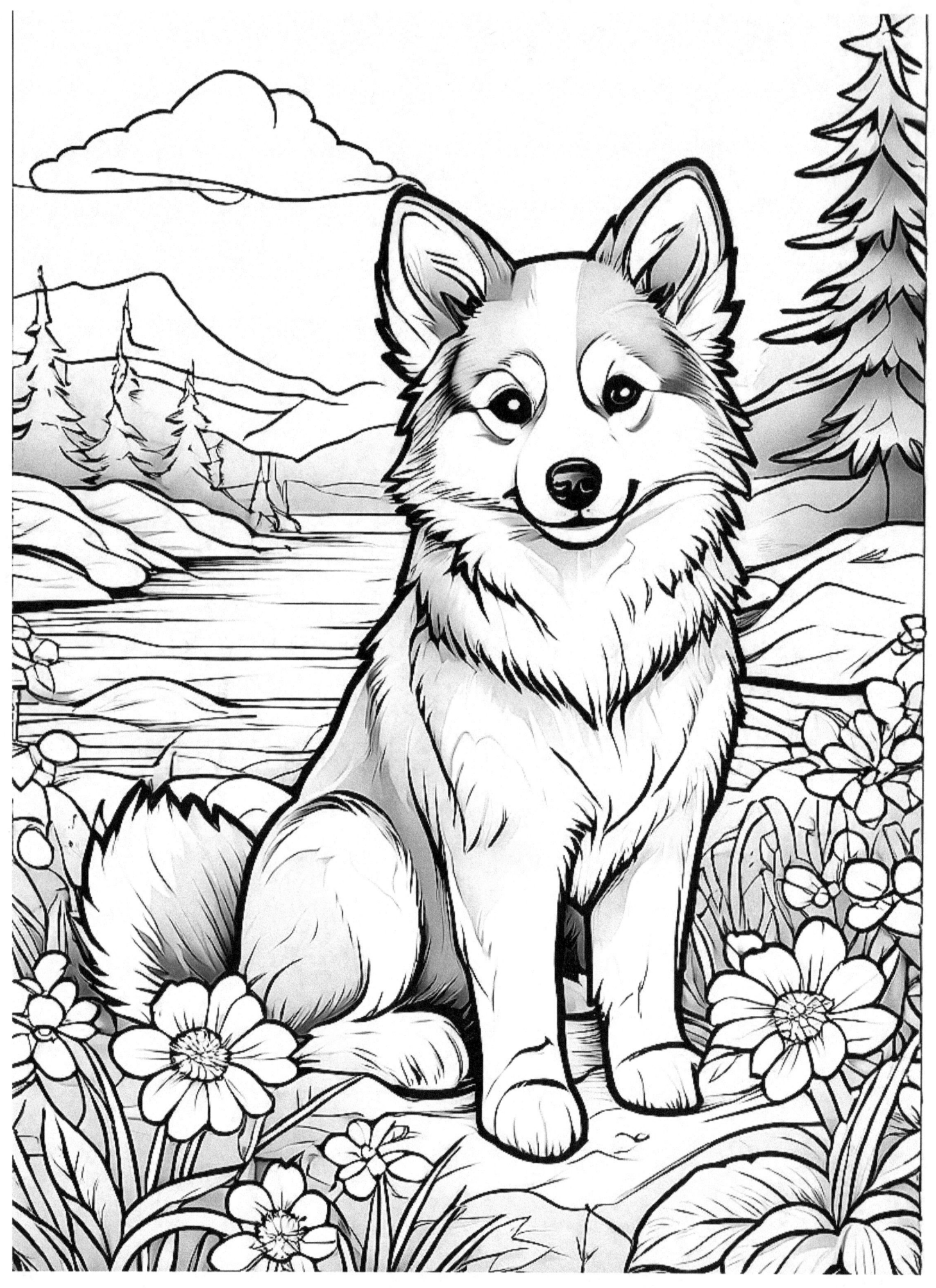

Akita Inu: Large, powerful, and noble with a thick coat. Origin: Japan. Weight: 32-59 kg. Lifespan: 10-15 years.

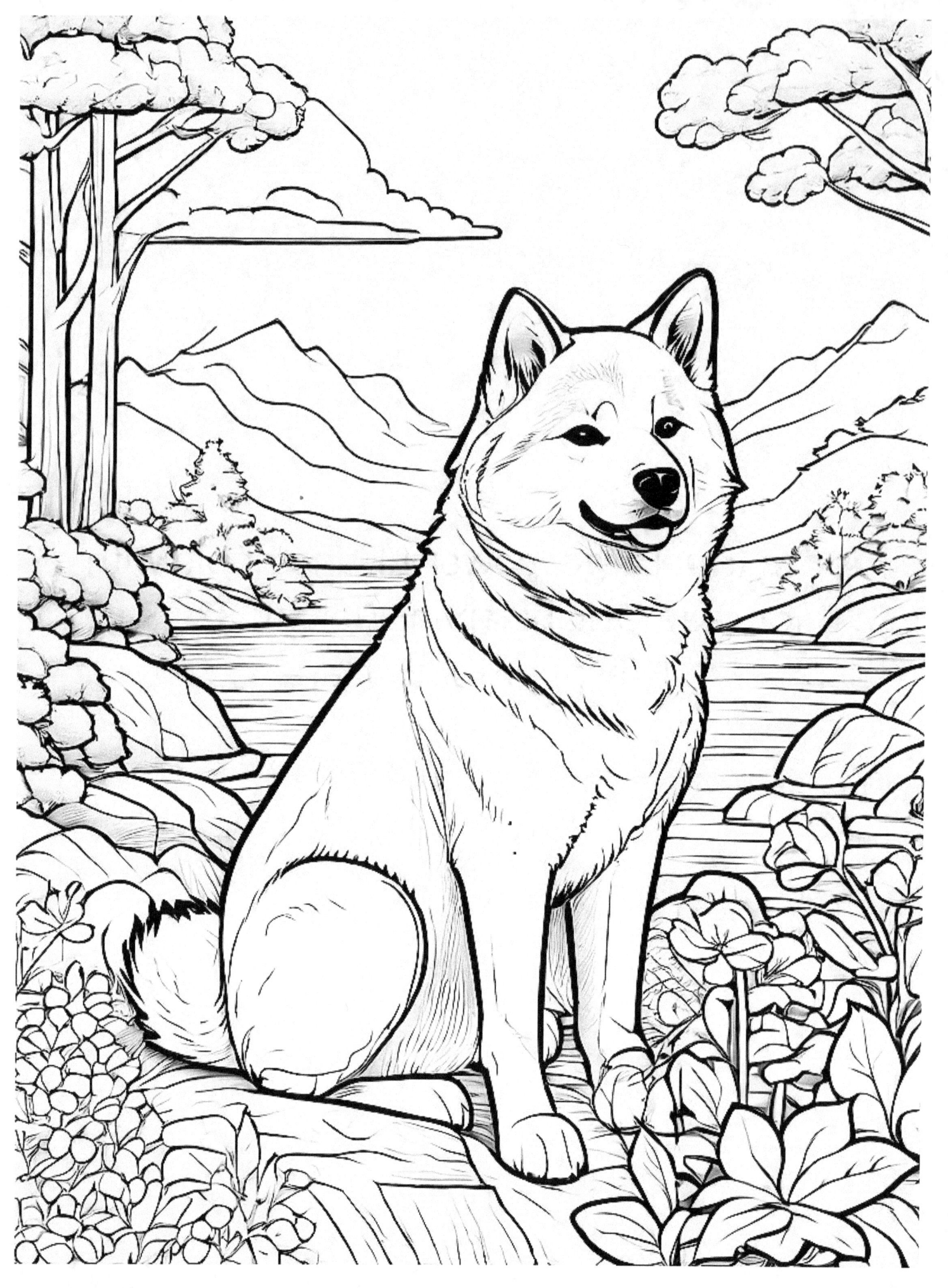

Beagle: Friendly, curious, and merry with a great sense of smell. Origin: United Kingdom. Weight: 9-11 kg. Lifespan: 12-15 years.

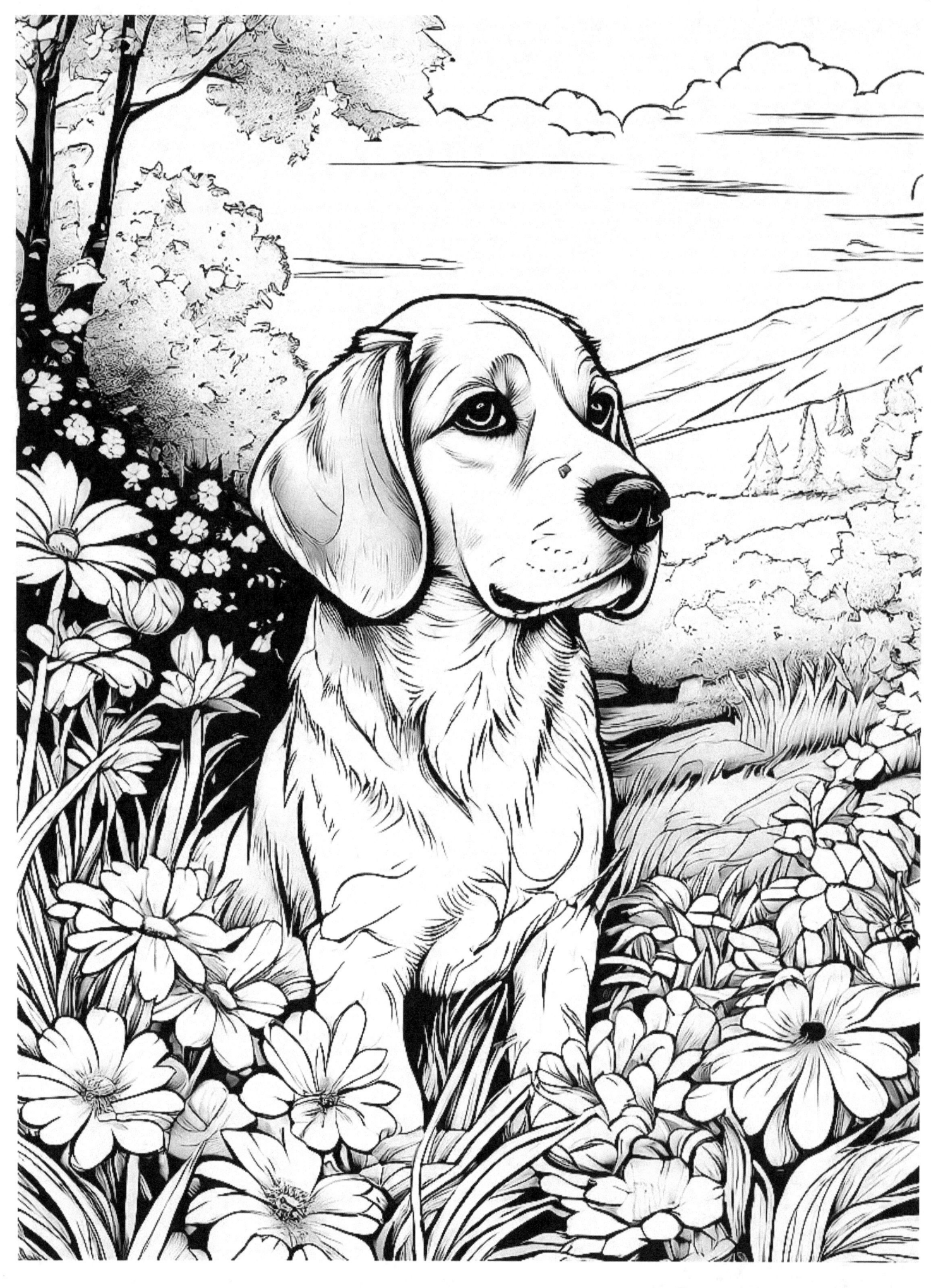

Alaskan Malamute: Strong, athletic, and affectionate. Origin: United States. Weight: 34-39 kg. Lifespan: 10-14 years.

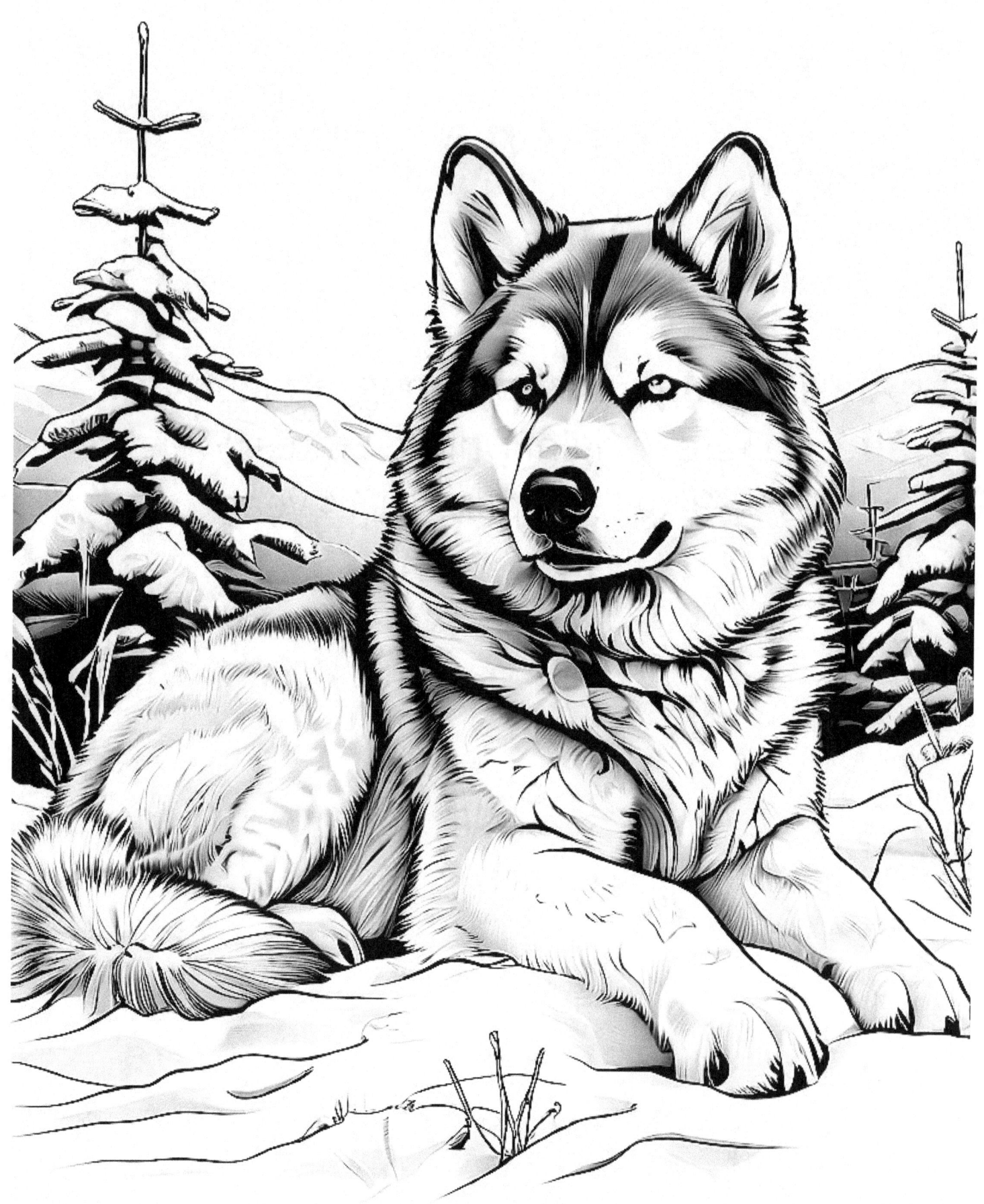

Afghan Hound: Elegant, with a long, flowing coat and dignified demeanor. Origin: Afghanistan. Weight: 20-27 kg. Lifespan: 12-18 years.

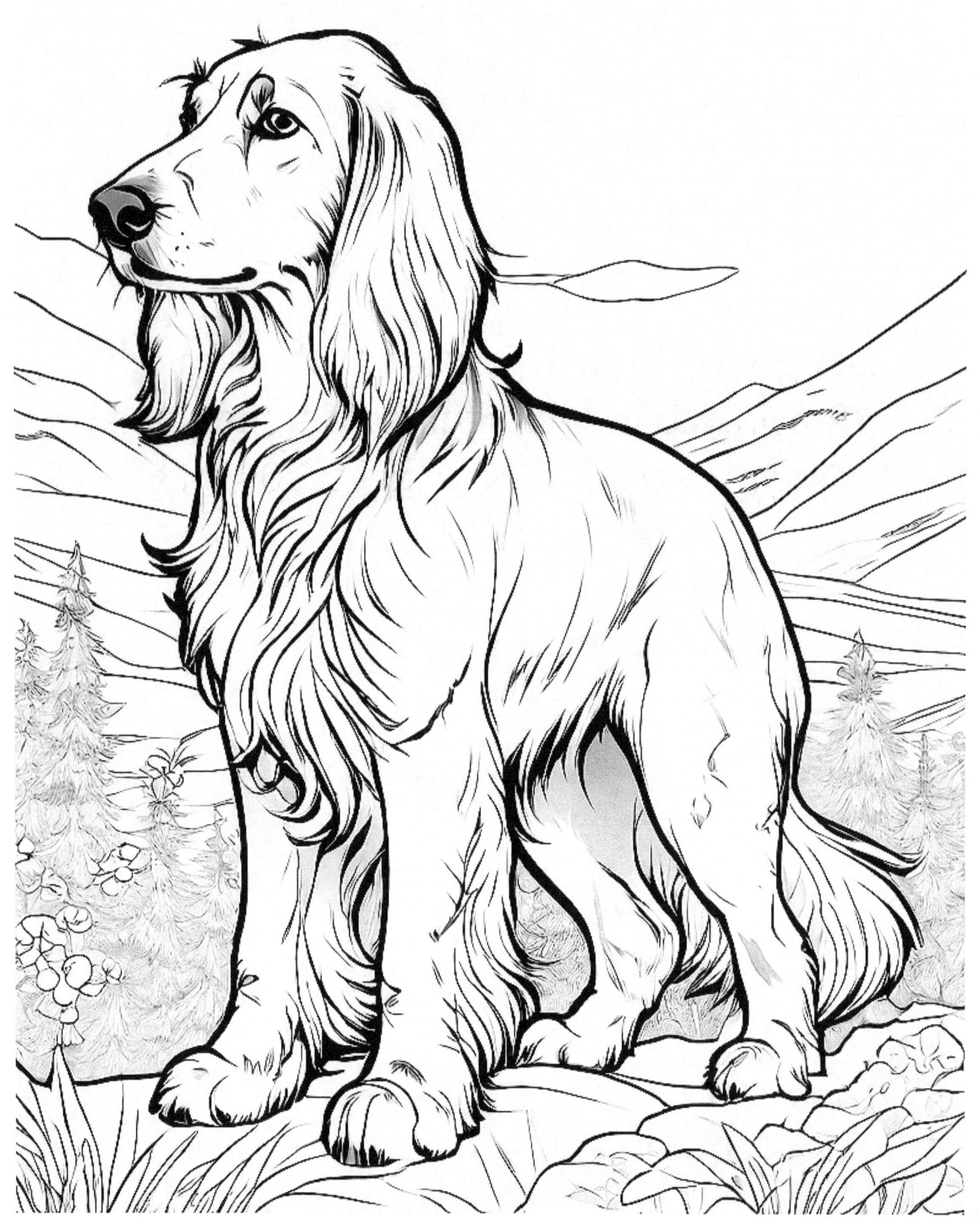

Border Collie: Highly intelligent, energetic, and excellent herders. Origin: United Kingdom. Weight: 12-20 kg. Lifespan: 12-15 years.

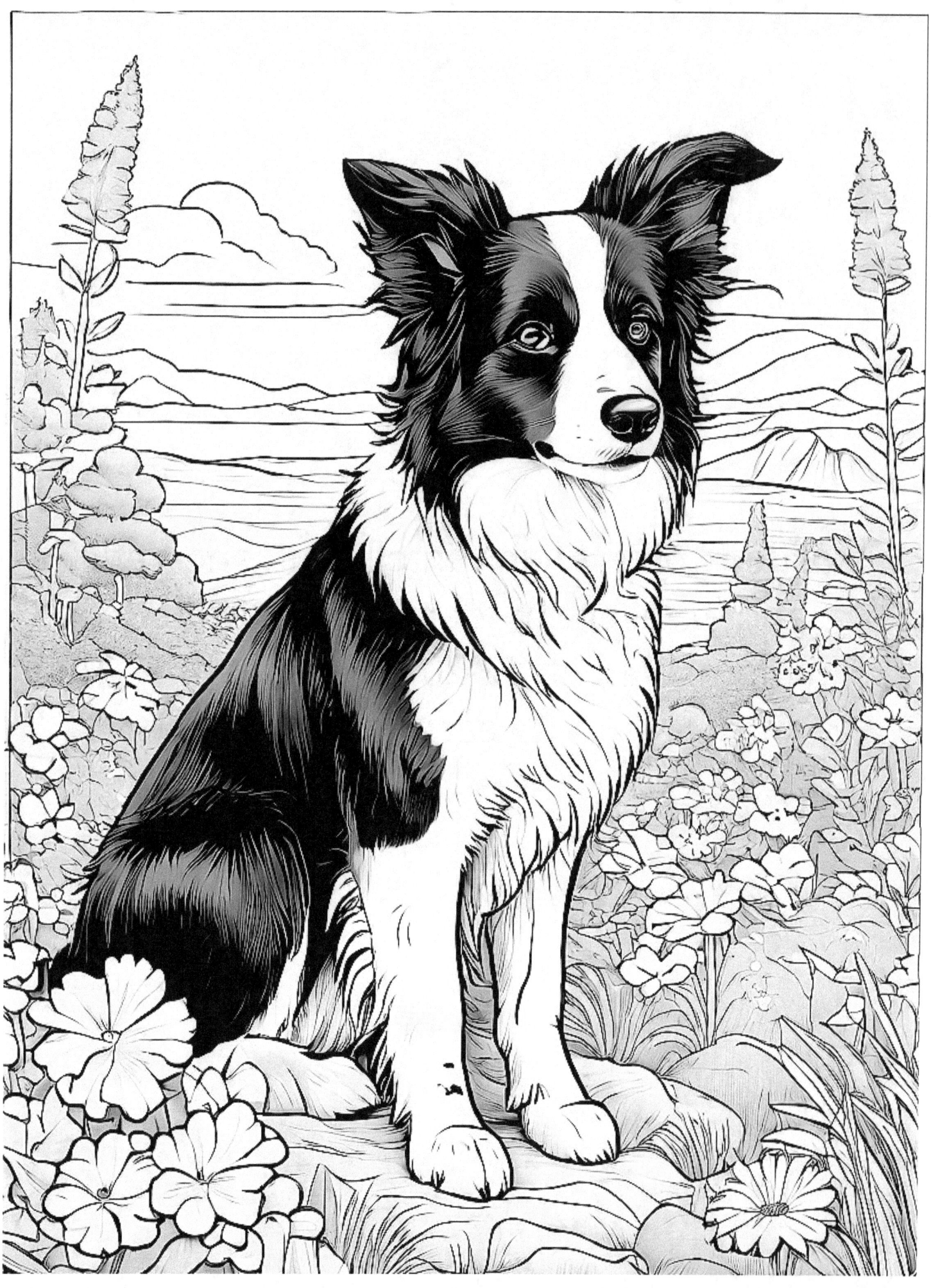

Bichon Frisé: Small, cheerful, and known for its fluffy white coat. Origin: France/Belgium. Weight: 5-10 kg. Lifespan: 12-15 years.

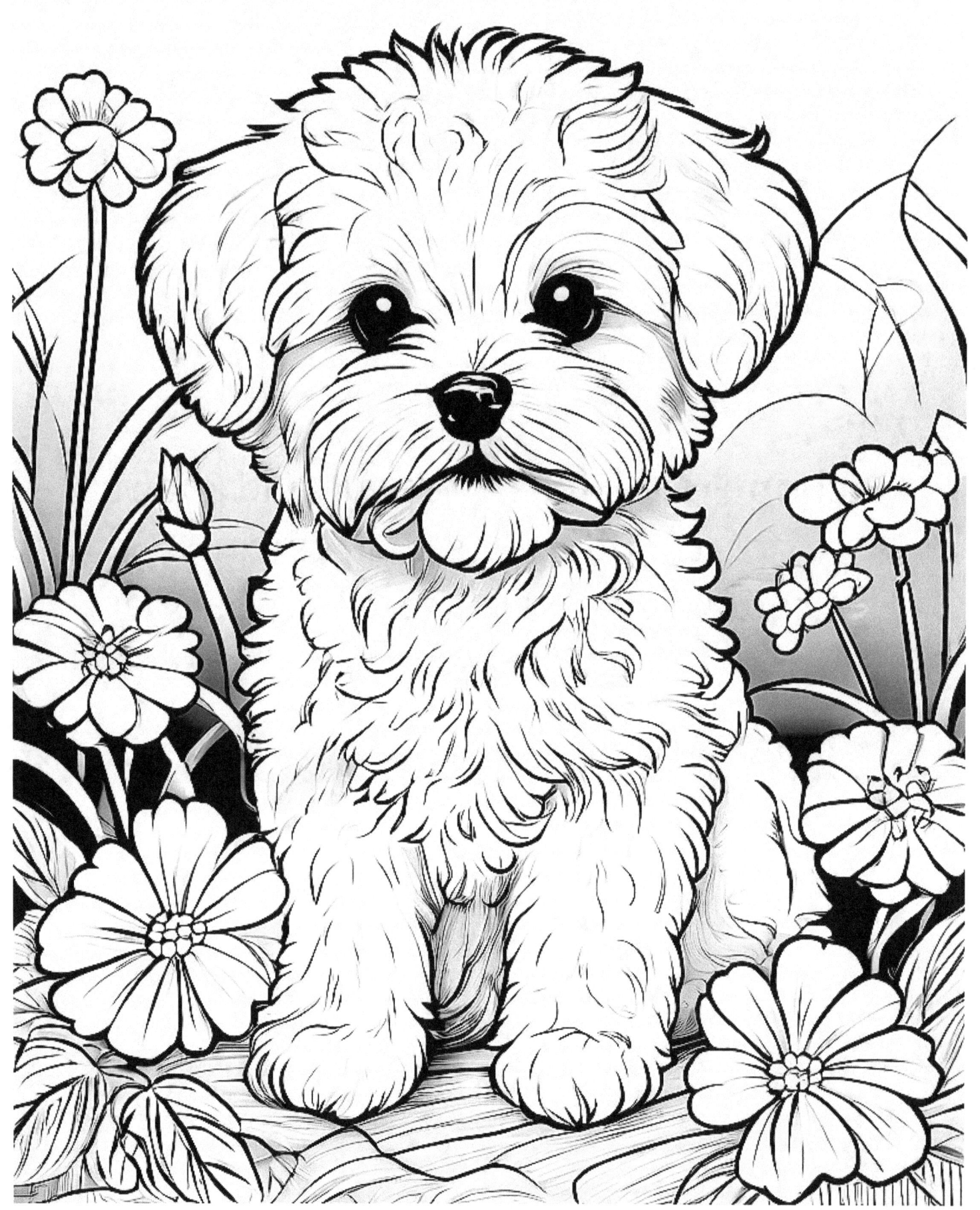

Borzoi: Graceful, elegant, and known for its long, silky coat. Origin: Russia. Weight: 27-48 kg. Lifespan: 9-14 years.

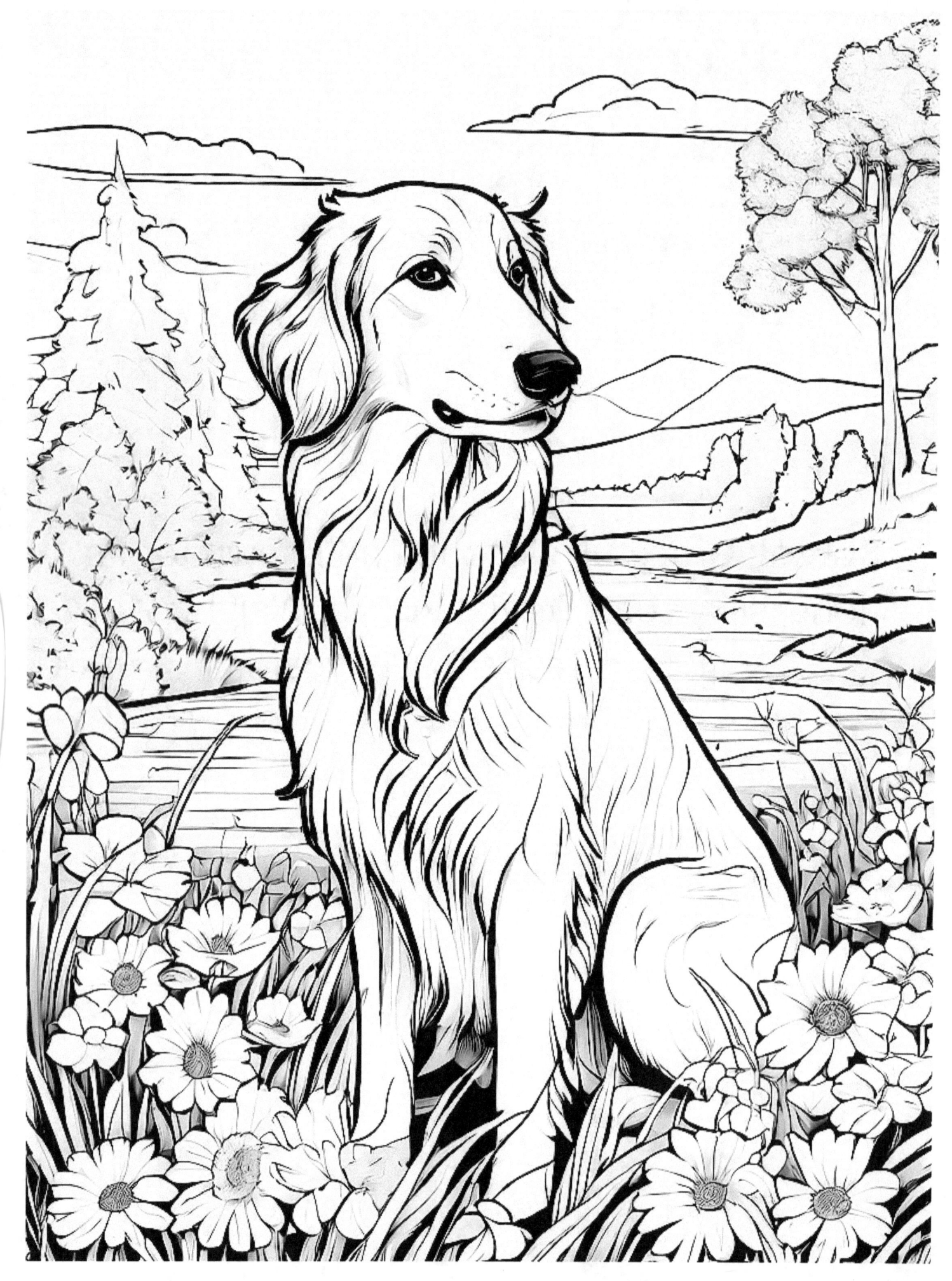

Bernese Mountain Dog: Large, gentle, and good-natured with a tri-color coat. Origin: Switzerland. Weight: 35-55 kg. Lifespan: 7-10 years.

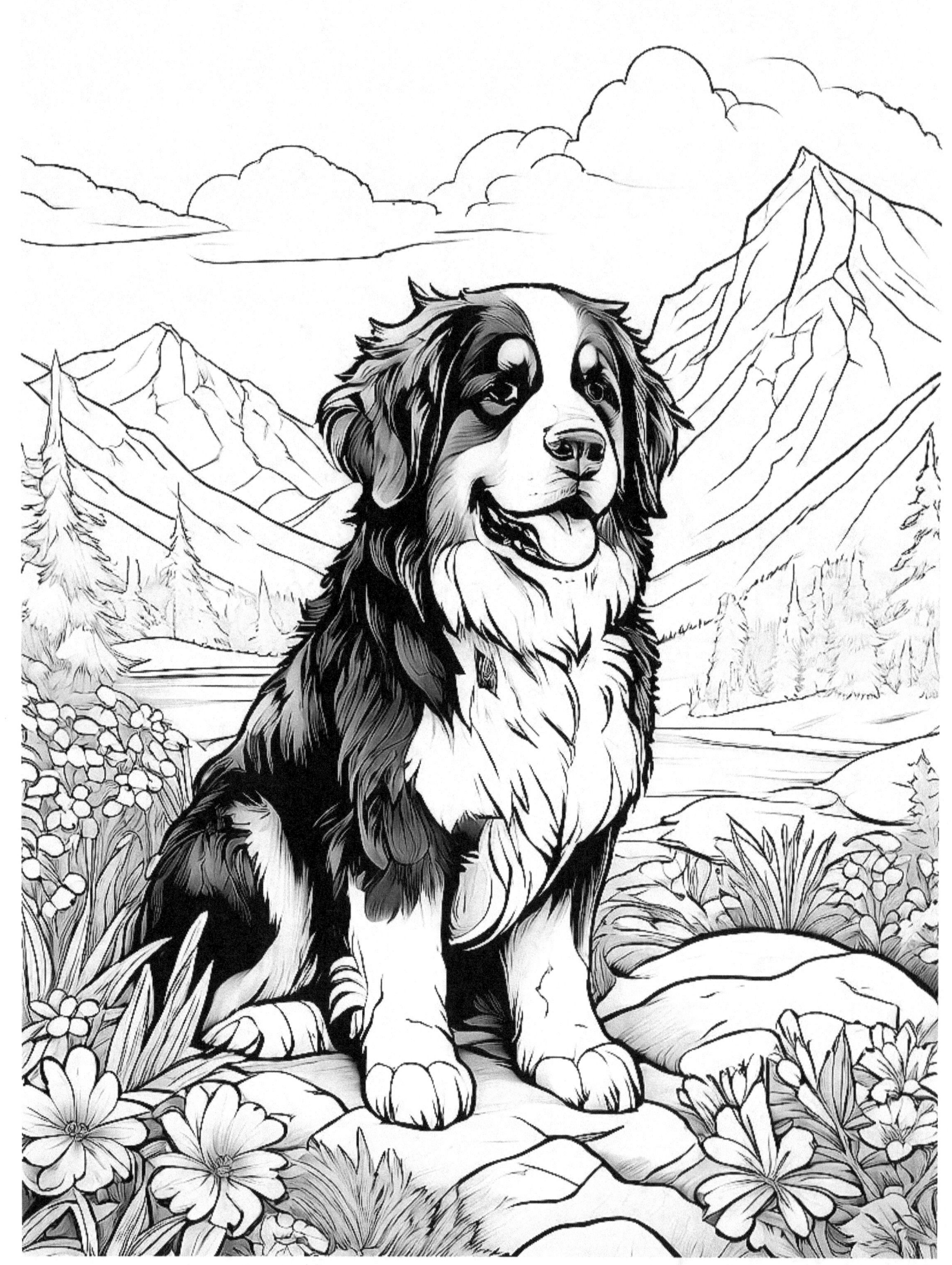

Australian Shepherd: Known for their beautiful merle coats and bright blue eyes. Origin: United States. Weight: 16-32 kg. Lifespan: 12-15 years.

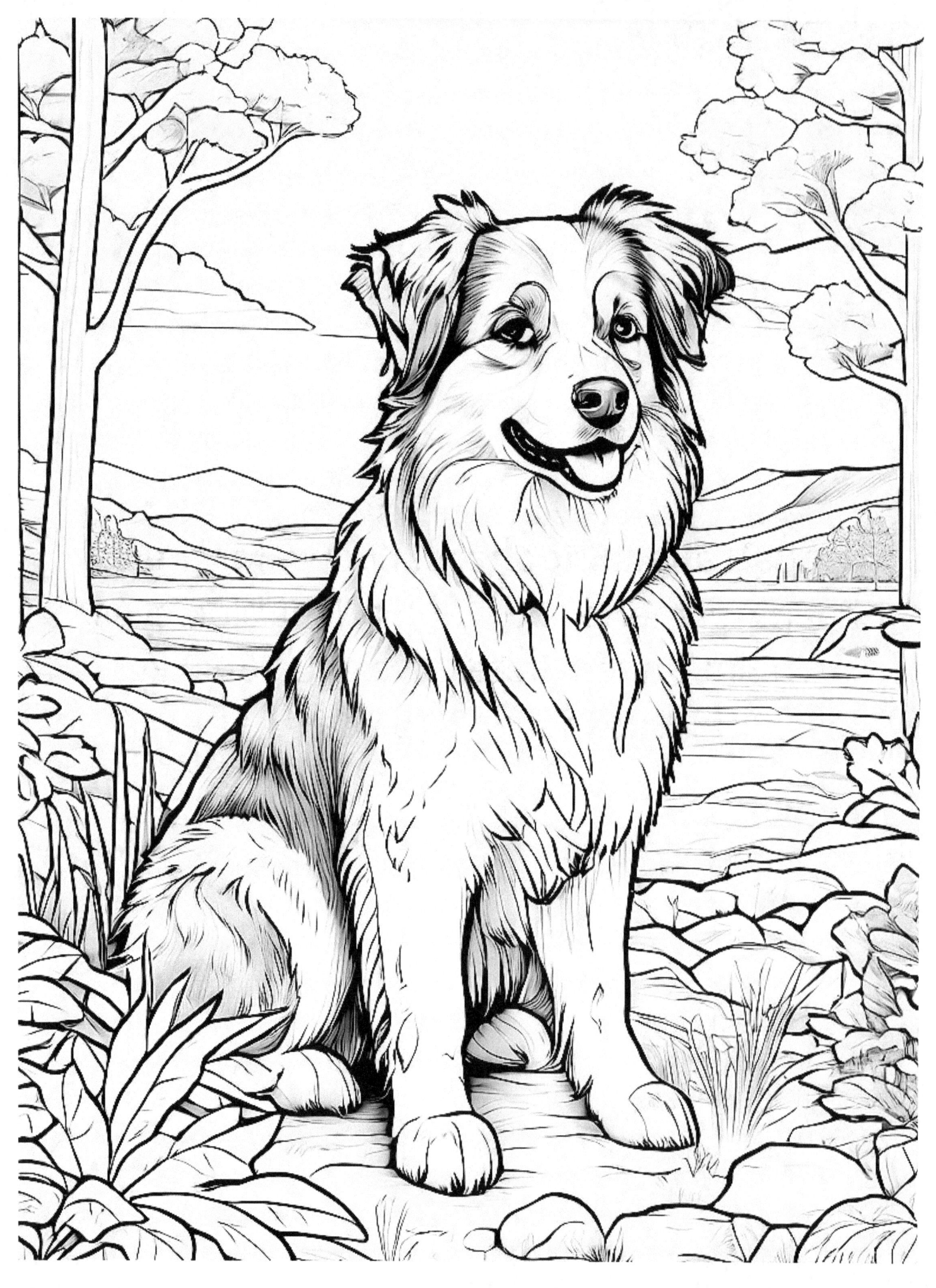

Doberman Pinscher: Elegant, powerful, and highly intelligent. Origin: Germany. Weight: 30-40 kg. Lifespan: 10-13 years.

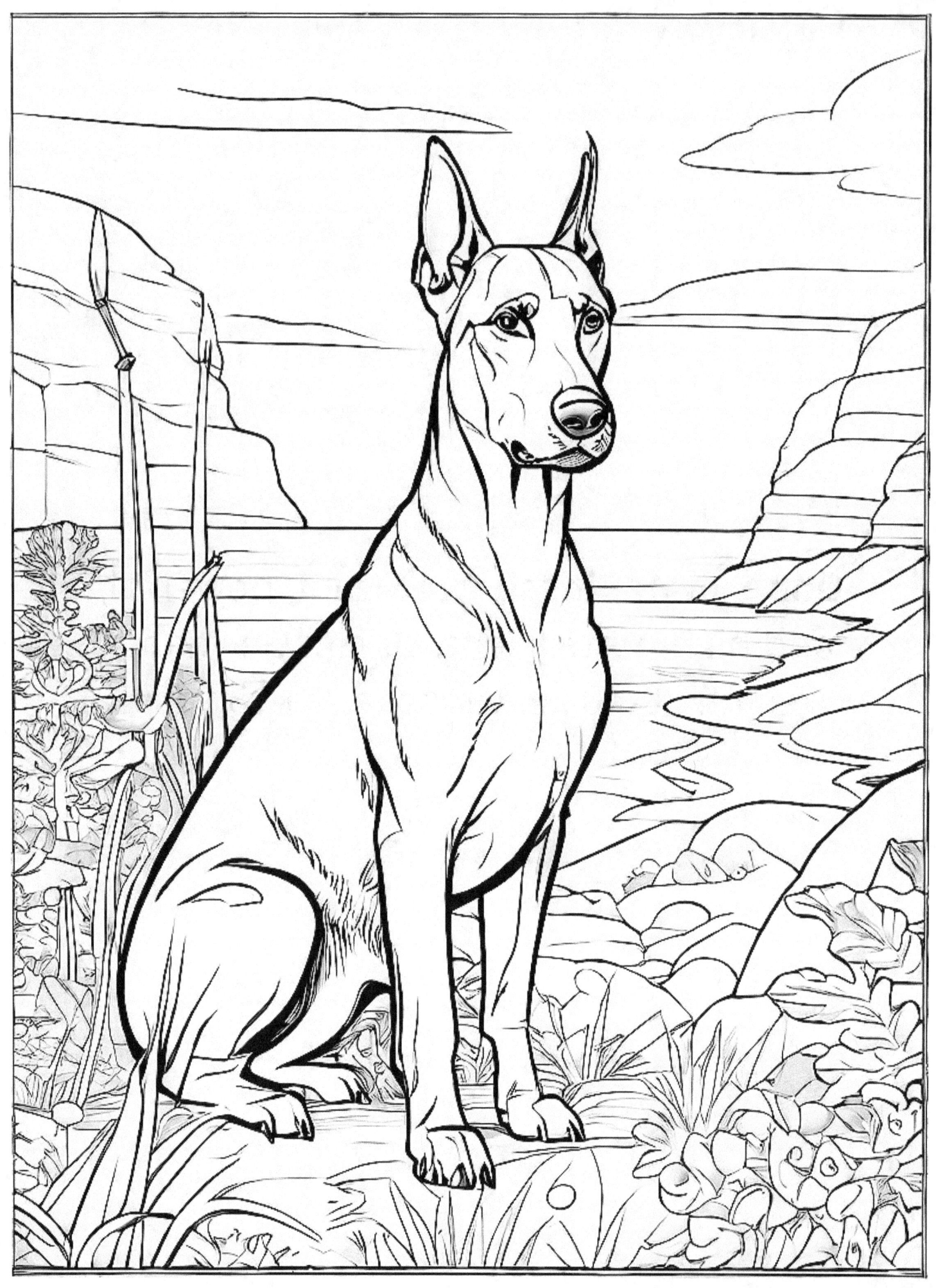

Chow Chow: Known for its lion-like mane and blue-black tongue. Origin: China. Weight: 20-32 kg. Lifespan: 9-15 years.

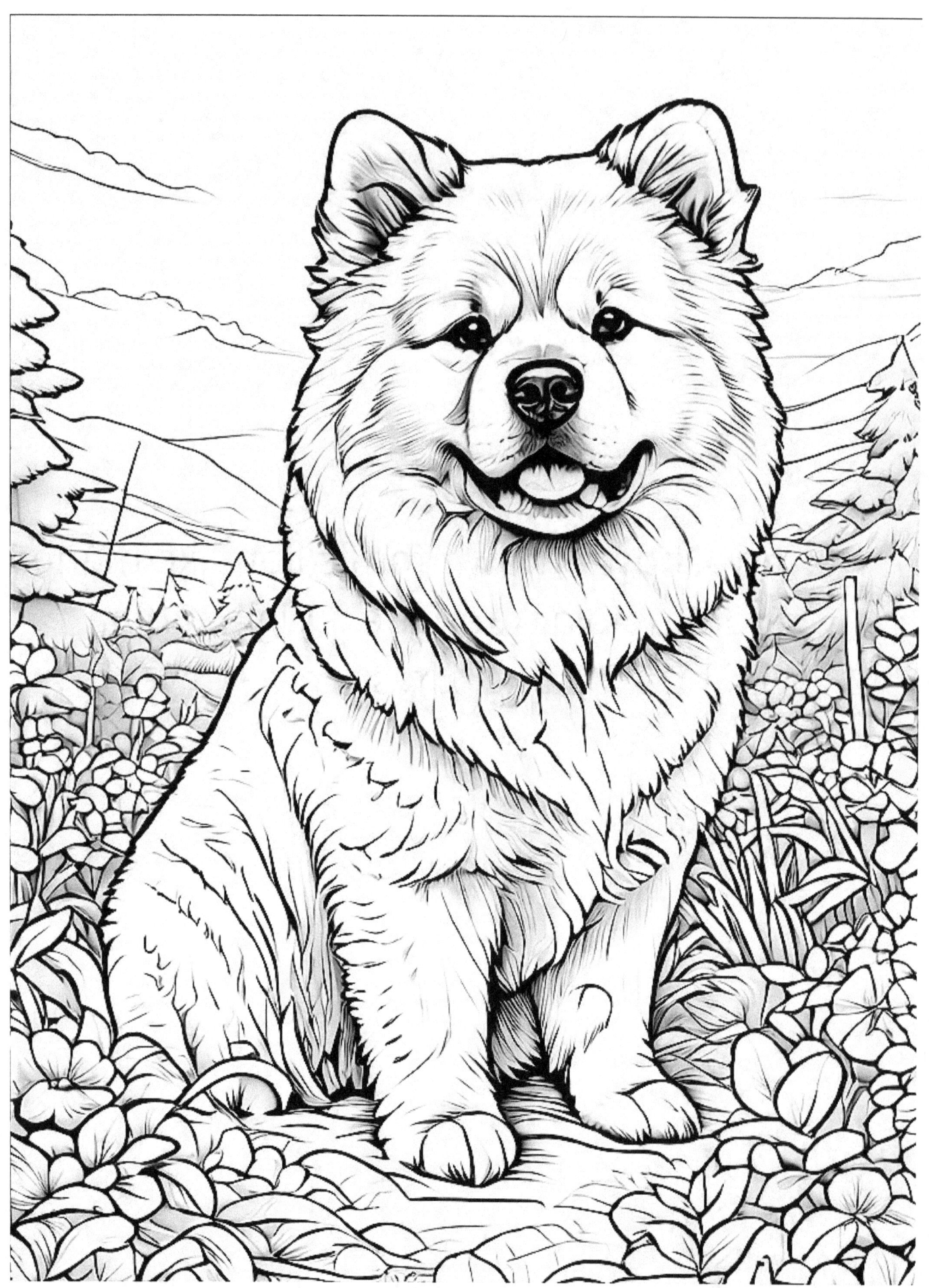

Boxer: Energetic, playful, and very loyal. Origin: Germany. Weight: 25-32 kg. Lifespan: 10-12 years.

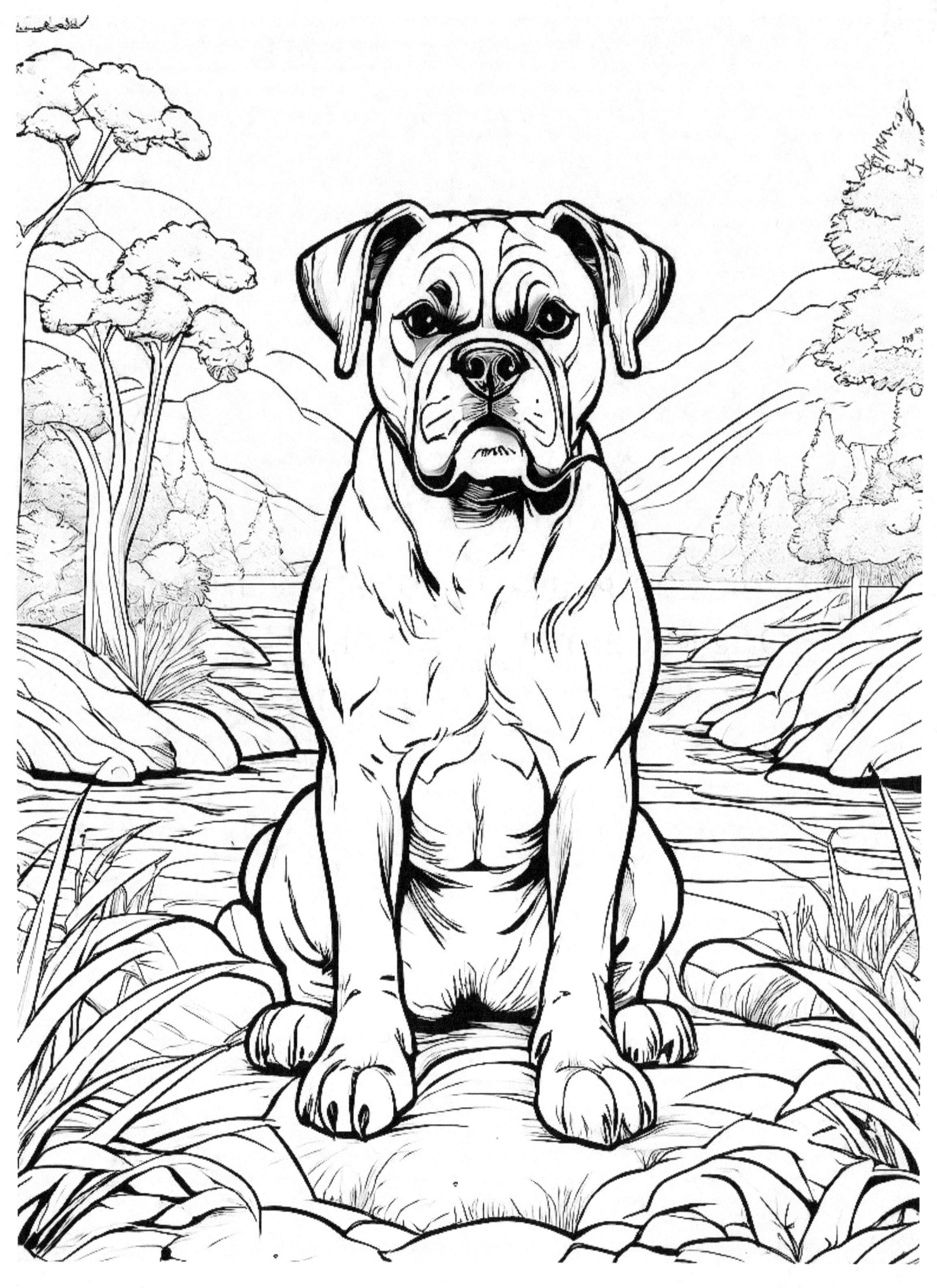

Brittany: A versatile and energetic breed with a soft, wavy coat and expressive eyes. Origin: France. Weight: 14-20 kg. Lifespan: 12-14 years.

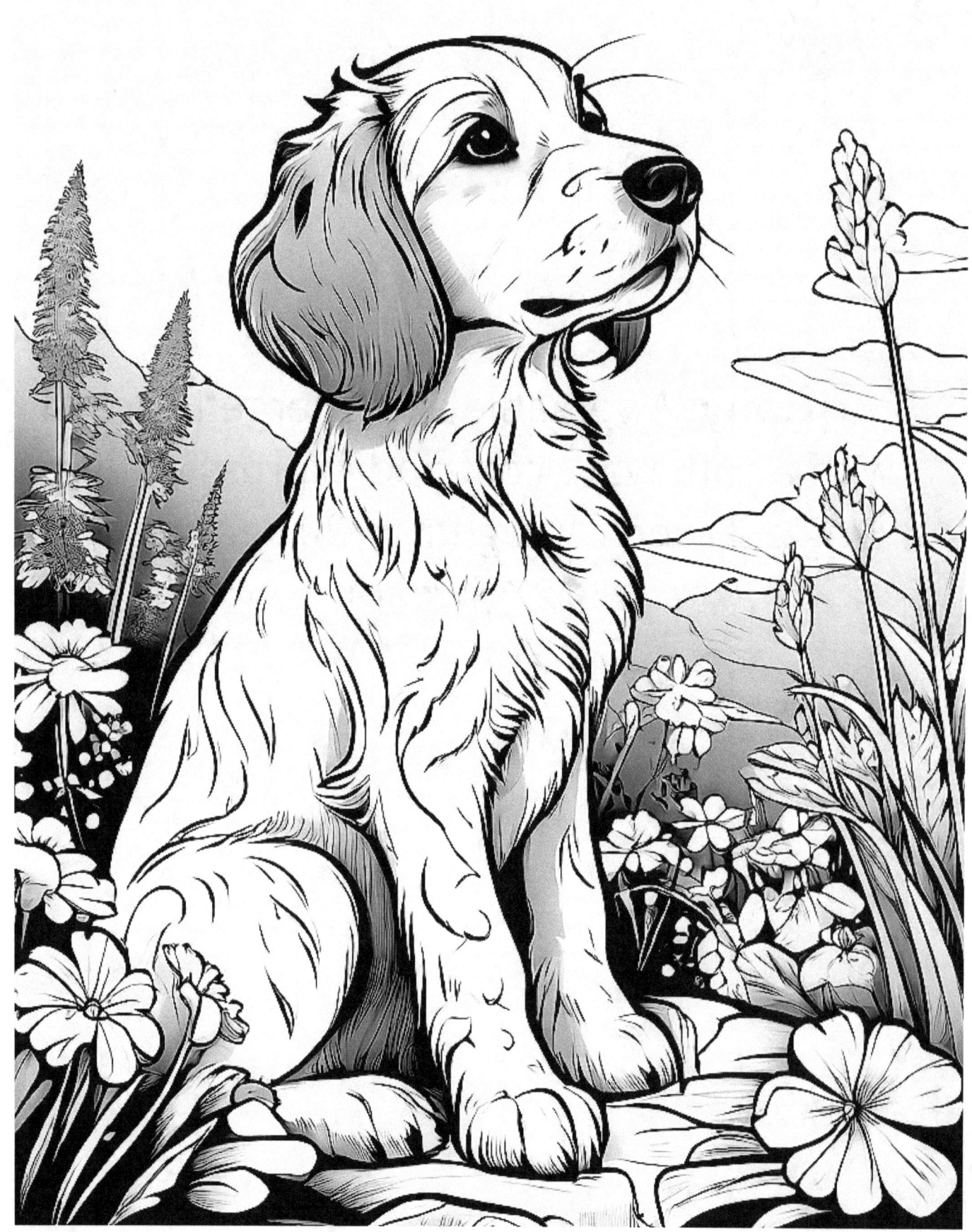

Cavalier King Charles Spaniel: Affectionate, graceful, and gentle. Origin: United Kingdom. Weight: 5-8 kg. Lifespan: 12-15 years.

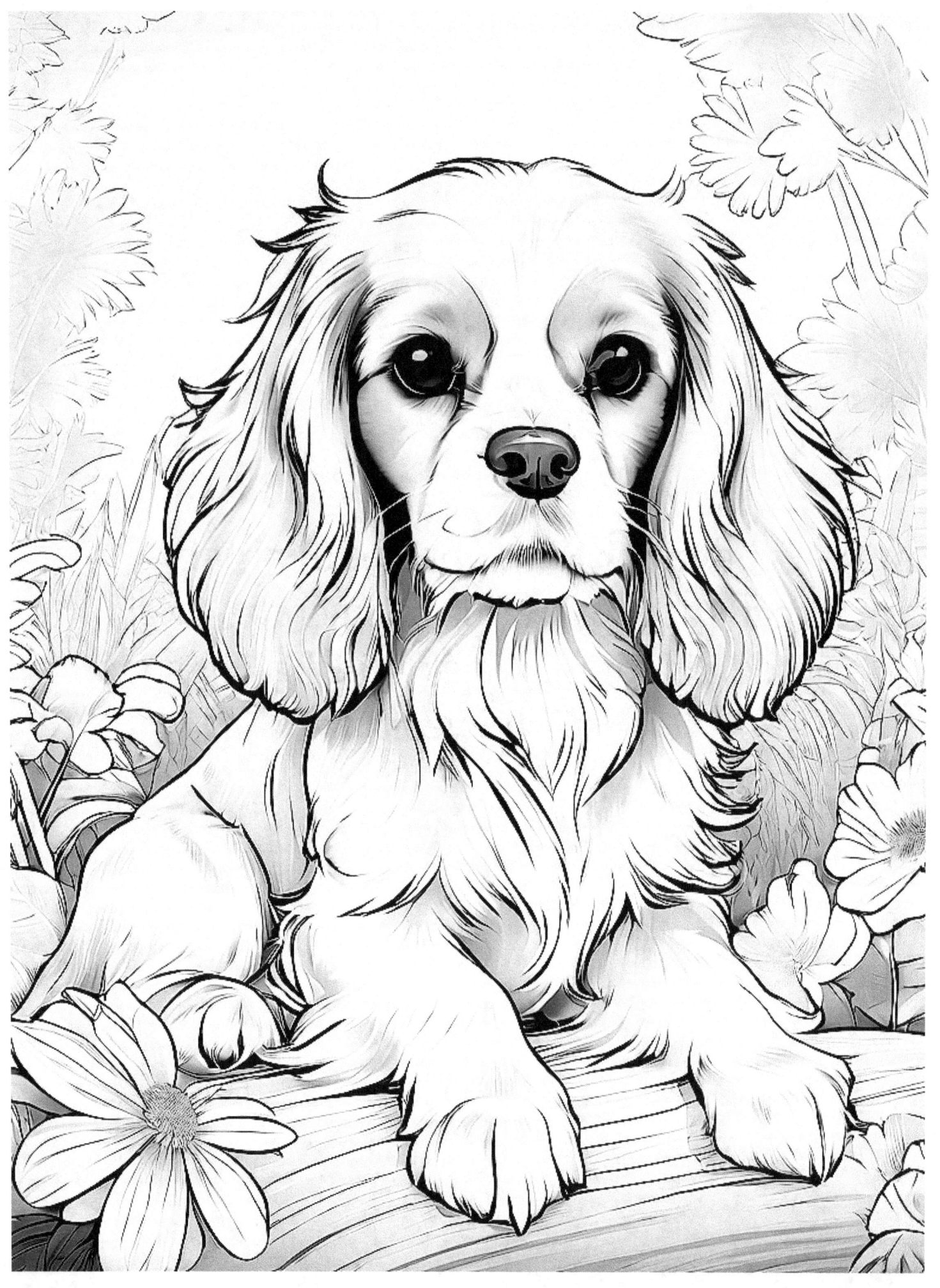

Cane Corso: A large and majestic breed with a powerful build and a short coat. Origin: Italy. Weight: 40-50 kg. Lifespan: 9-12 years.

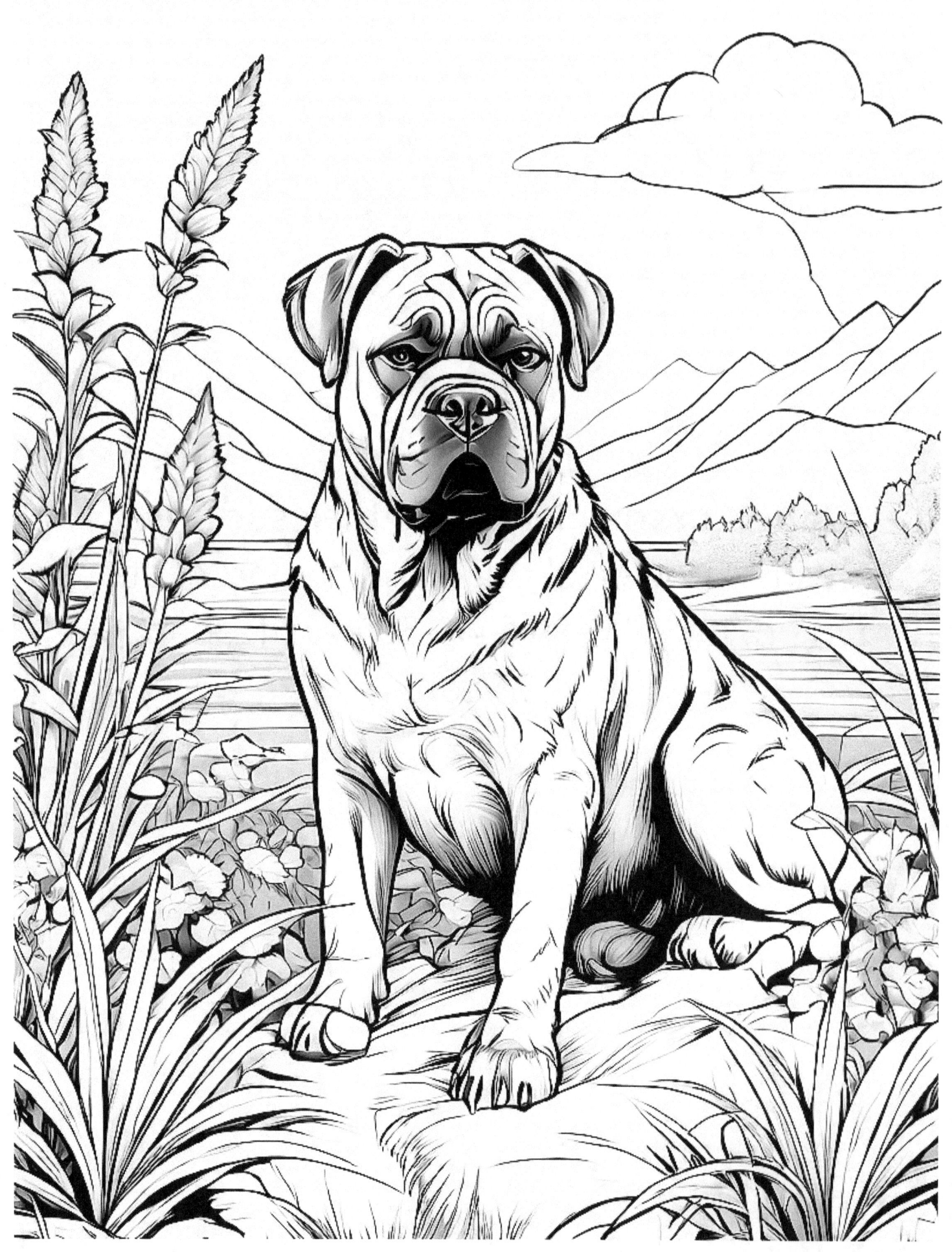

Boston Terrier: Small, compact, and friendly with a tuxedo-like coat. Origin: United States. Weight: 4.5-11 kg. Lifespan: 11-13 years.

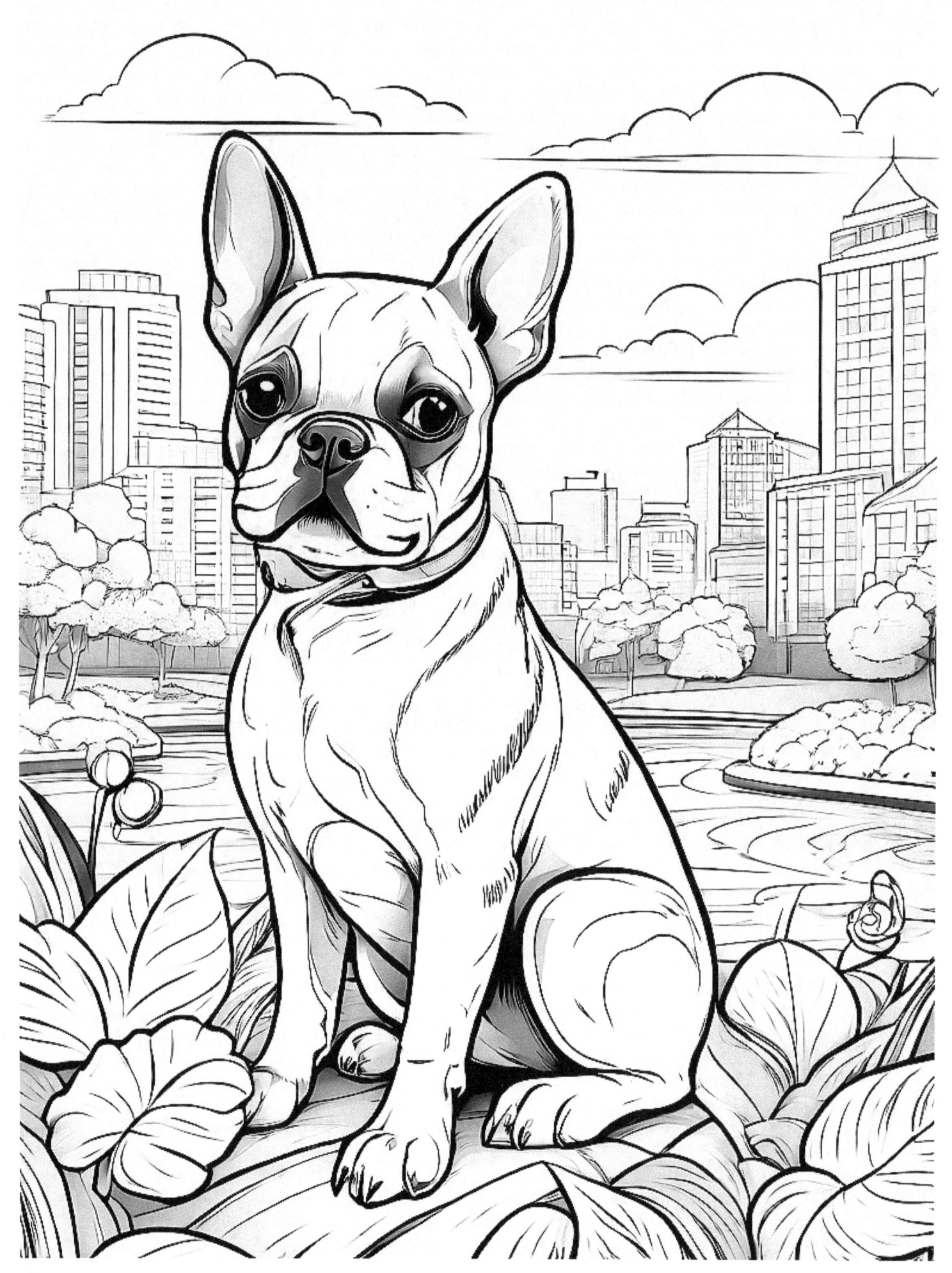

Dalmatian: Known for its unique black or liver spotted coat. Origin: Croatia. Weight: 16-32 kg. Lifespan: 10-13 years.

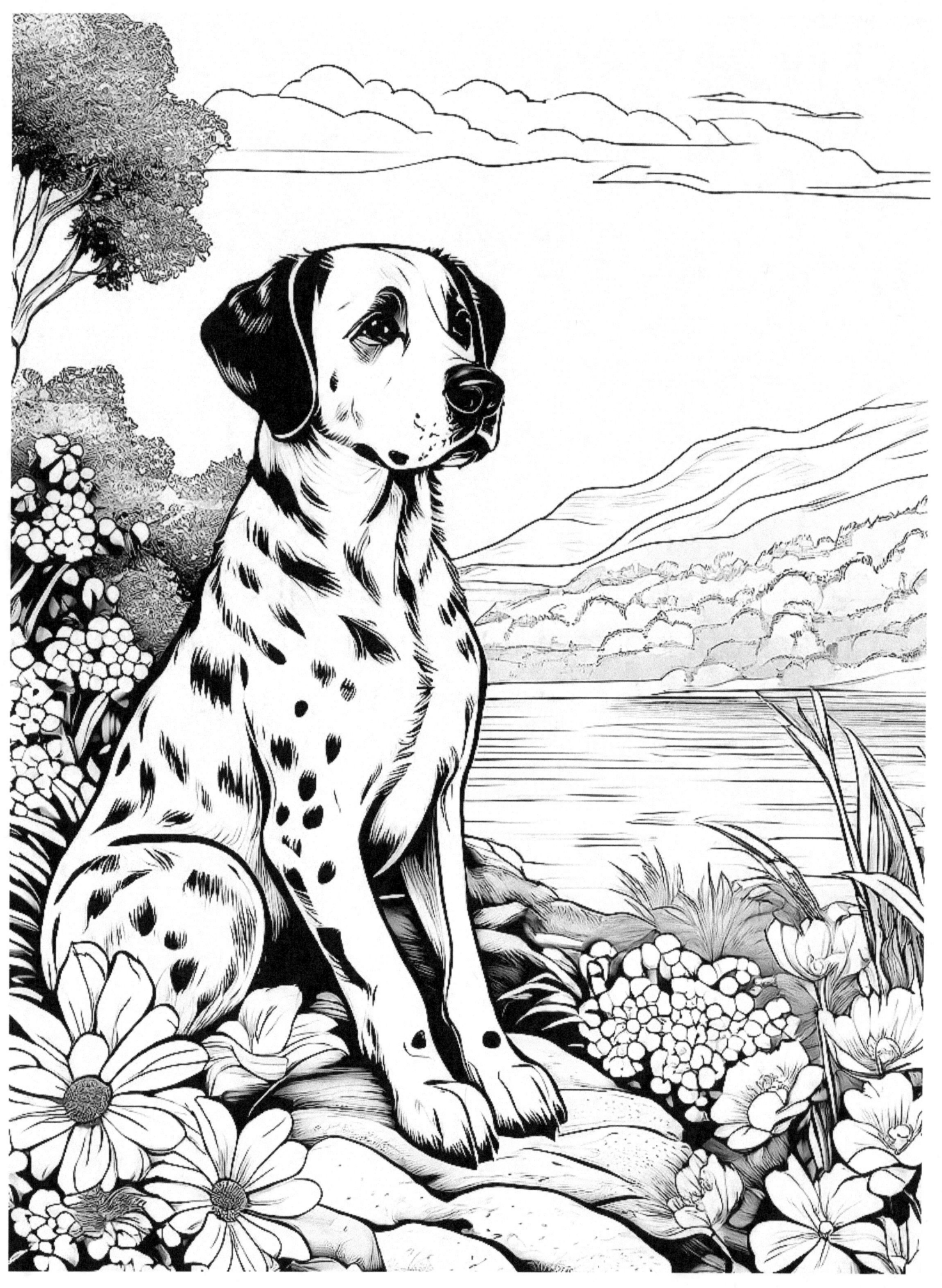

Collie: Graceful, intelligent, and devoted. Origin: Scotland. Weight: 18-30 kg. Lifespan: 12-14 years.

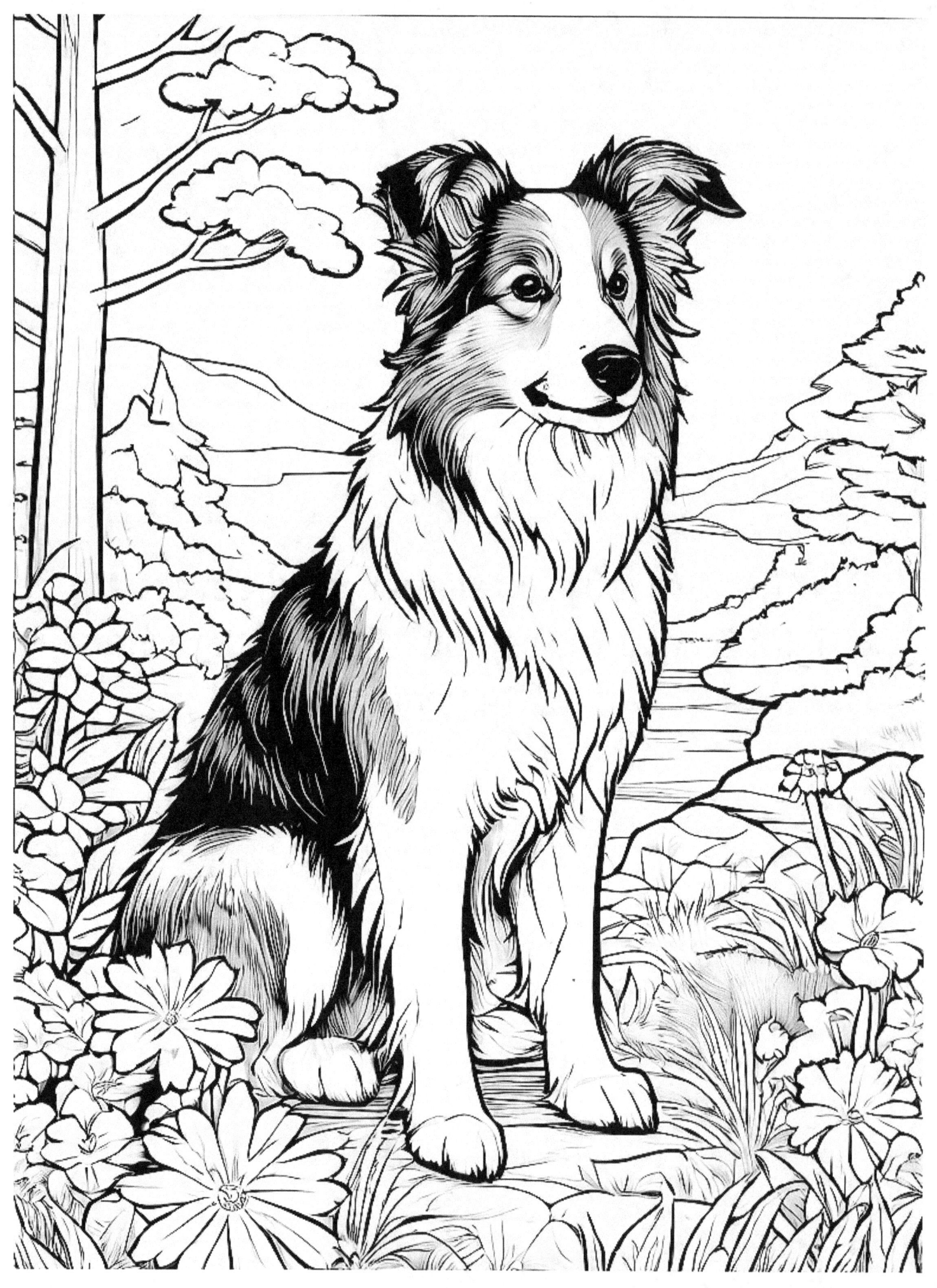

Chinese Crested: Small, with unique hairless or powderpuff coat varieties. Origin: China. Weight: 2.3-5.4 kg. Lifespan: 13-18 years.

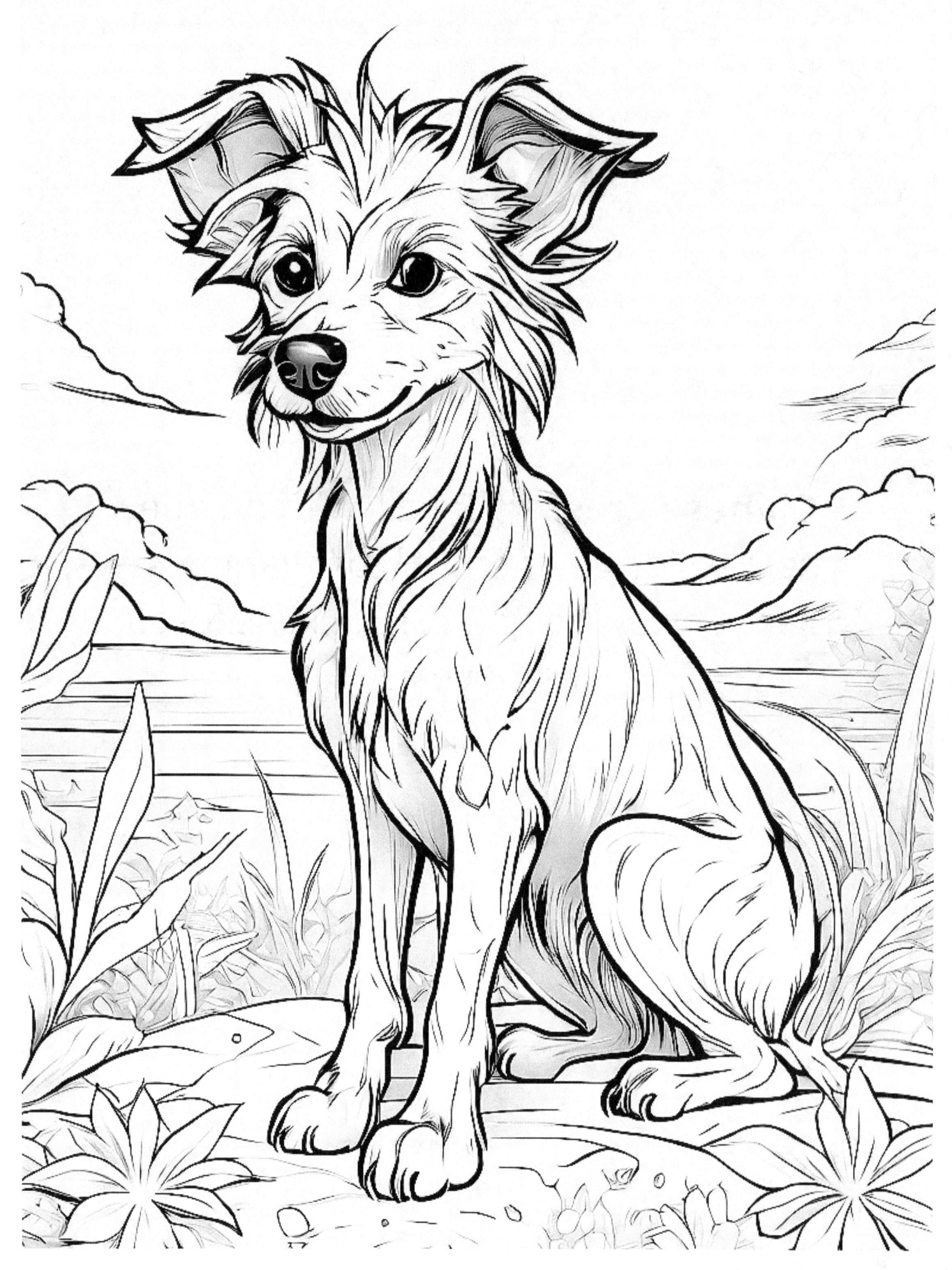

Irish Setter: Known for its stunning red coat and playful nature. Origin: Ireland. Weight: 25-34 kg. Lifespan: 12-15 years.

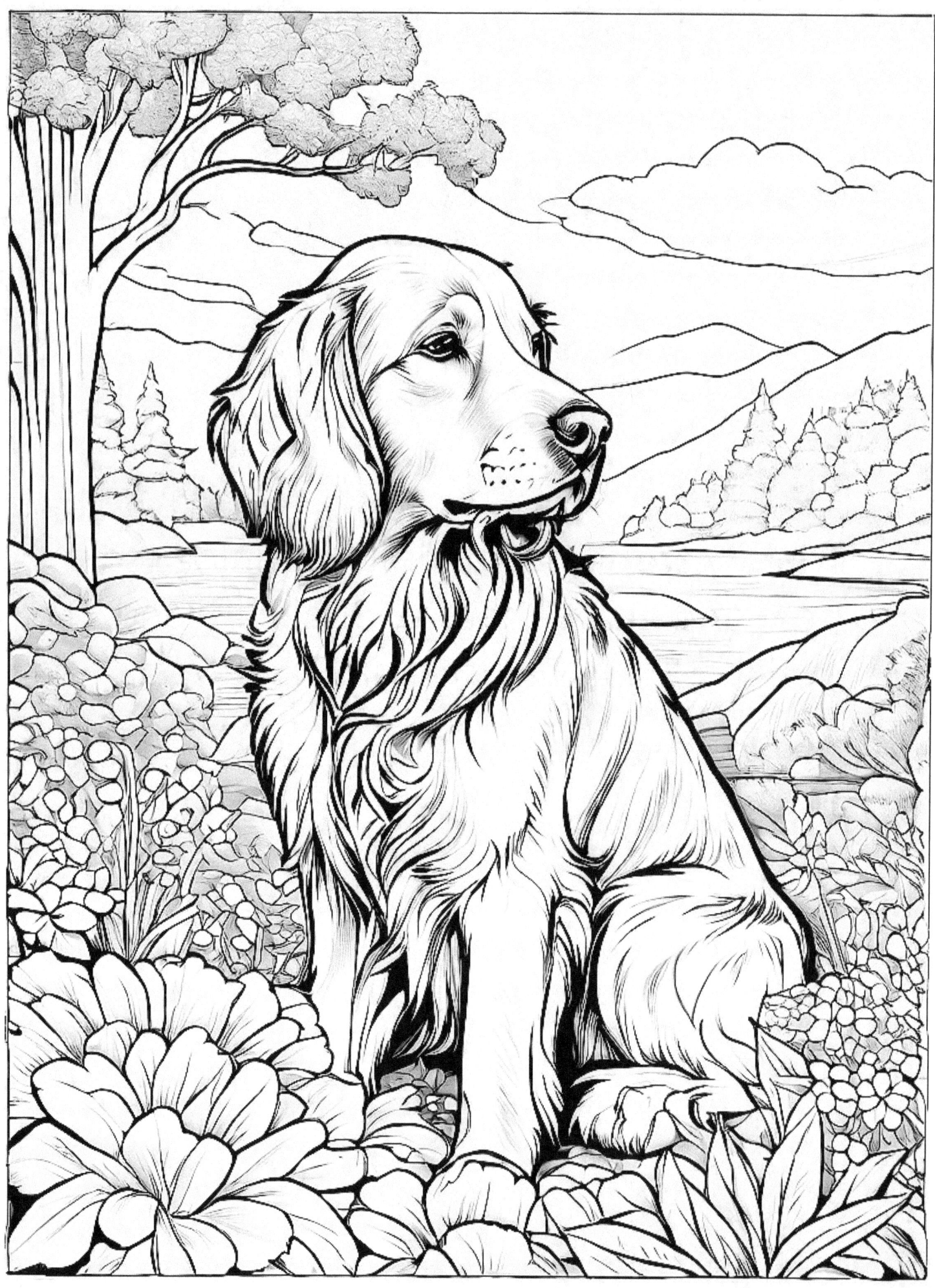

Italian Greyhound: Small, slender, and elegant with a gentle nature. Origin: Italy. Weight: 3.6-4.5 kg. Lifespan: 14-15 years.

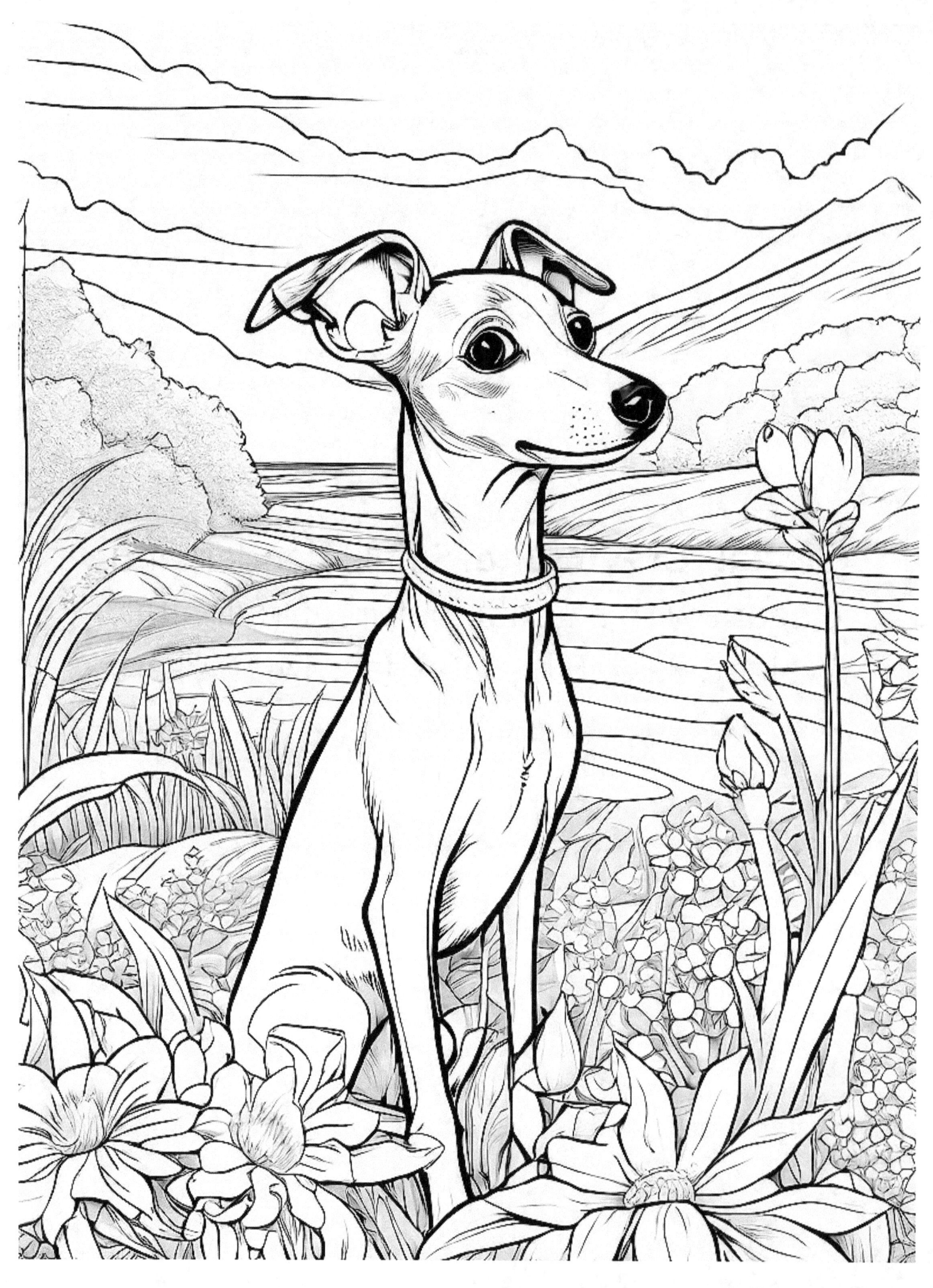

Labrador Retriever: Loyal, friendly, and great with families. Origin: Canada. Weight: 25-36 kg. Lifespan: 10-12 years.

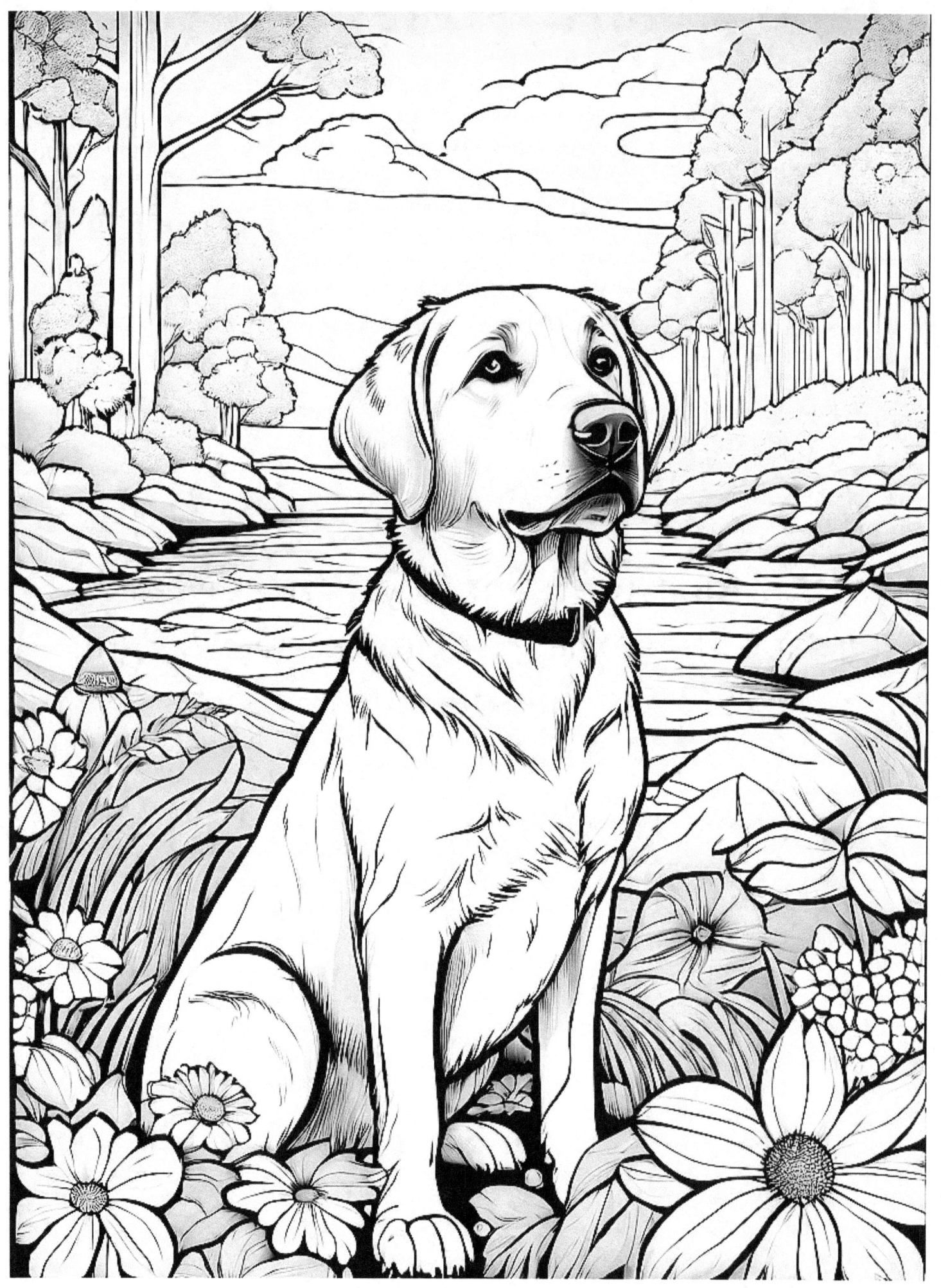

English Springer Spaniel: Friendly, energetic, and excellent hunting companion. Origin: United Kingdom. Weight: 18-25 kg. Lifespan: 12-14 years.

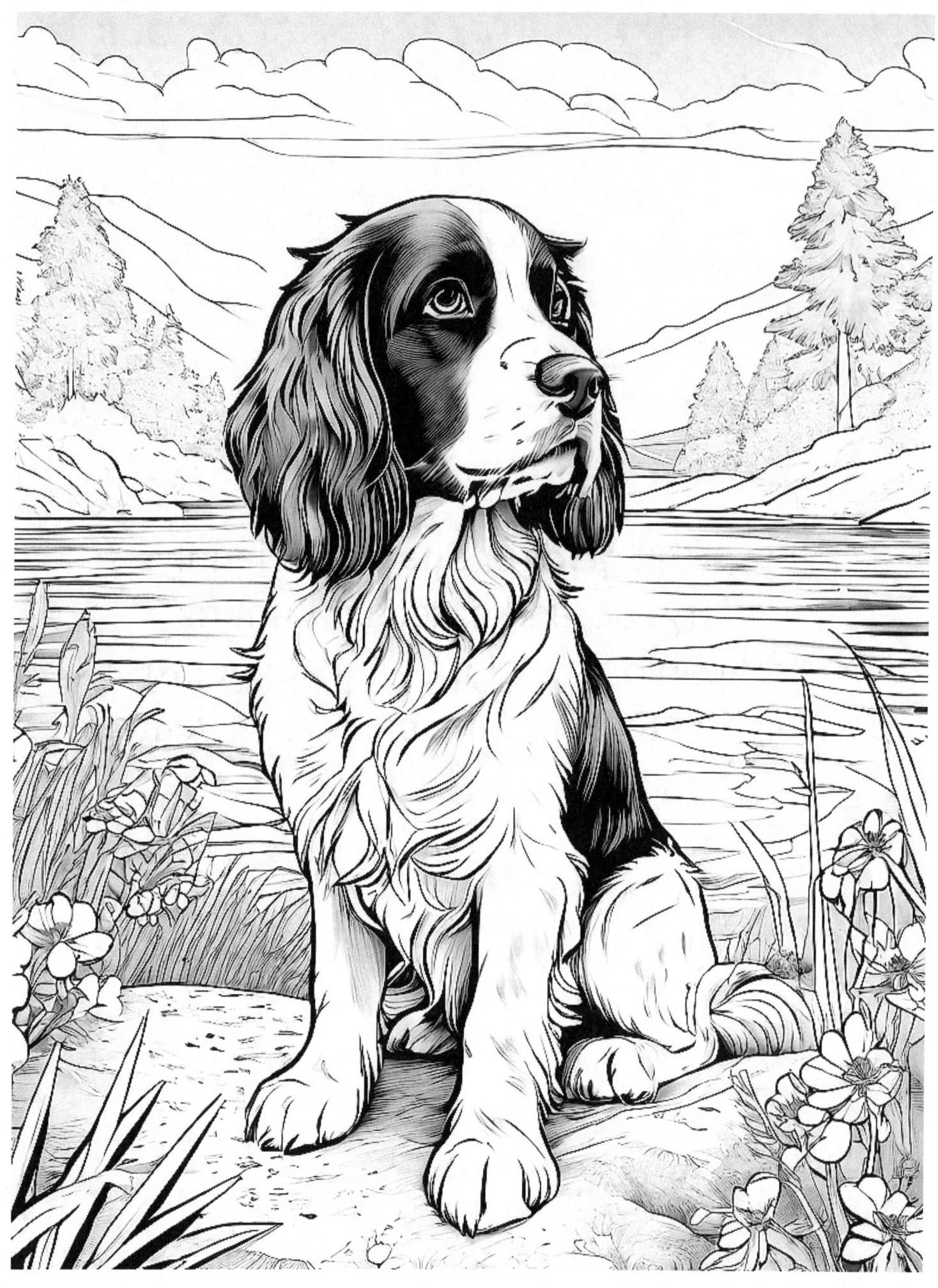

Lhasa Apso: Small, with a long, flowing coat and alert nature. Origin: Tibet. Weight: 5-8 kg. Lifespan: 12-15 years.

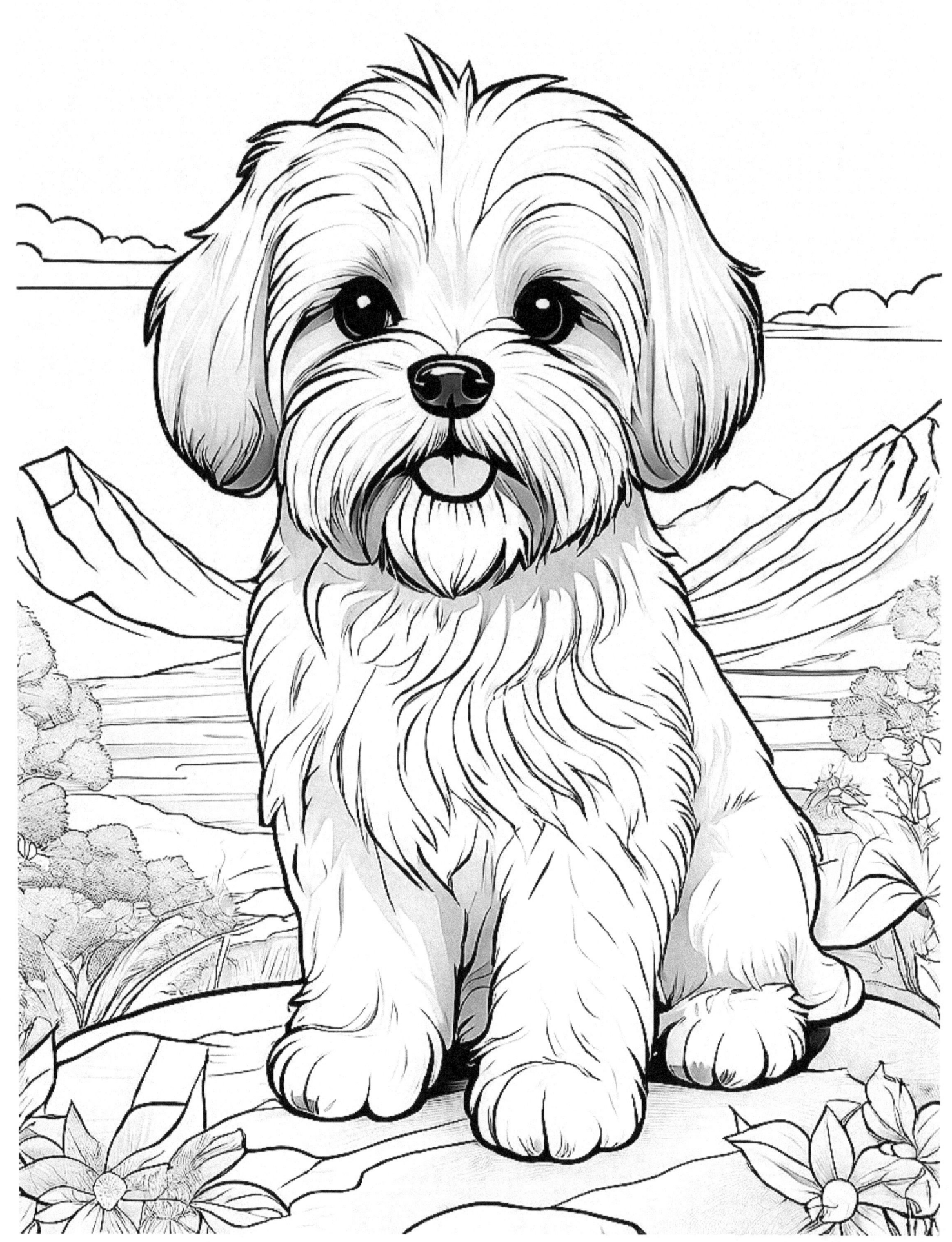

German Shepherd: Highly intelligent and versatile working dog. Origin: Germany. Weight: 22-40 kg. Lifespan: 9-13 years.

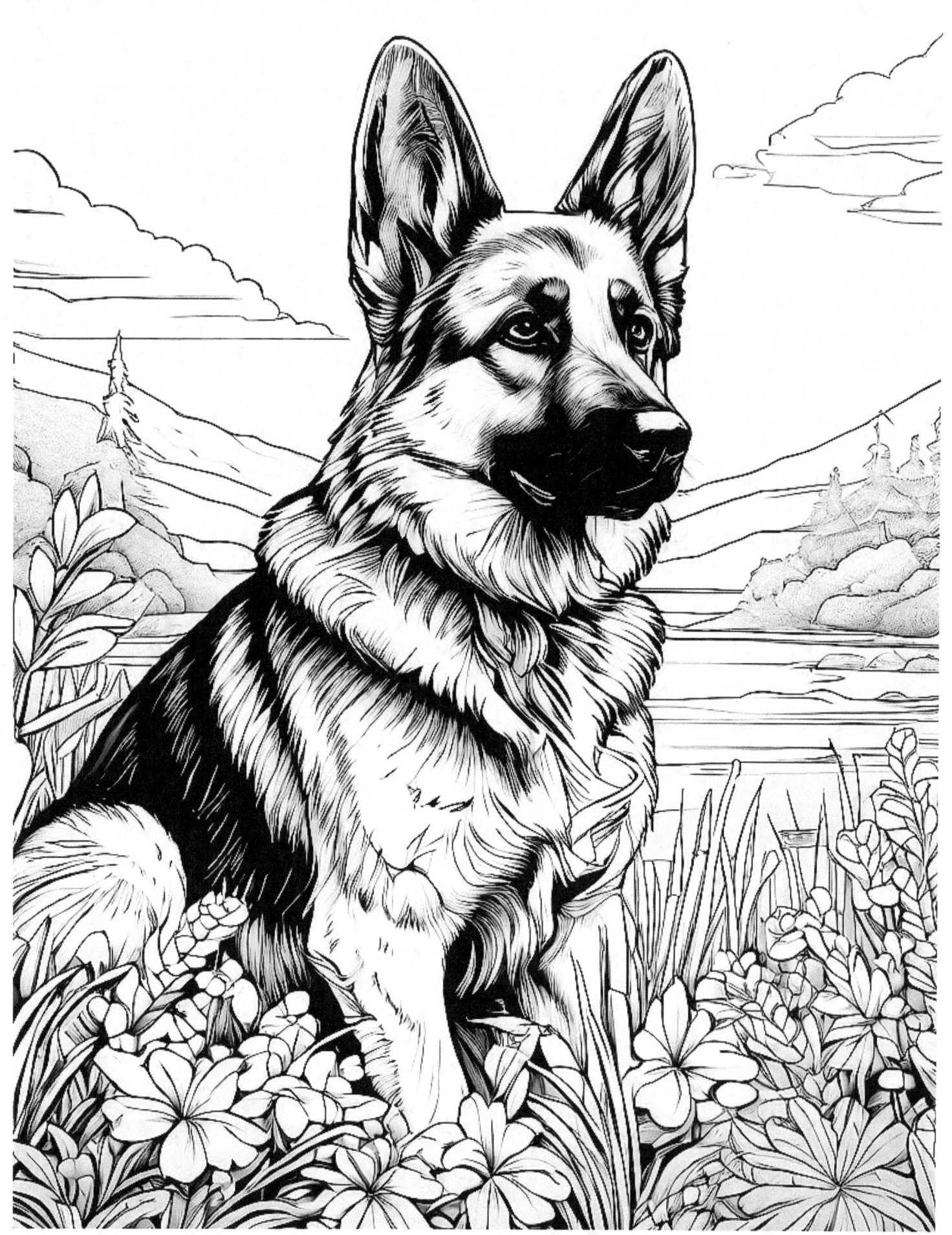

French Bulldog: Small, muscular with a smooth coat and bat-like ears. Origin: France. Weight: 9-13 kg. Lifespan: 10-12 years.

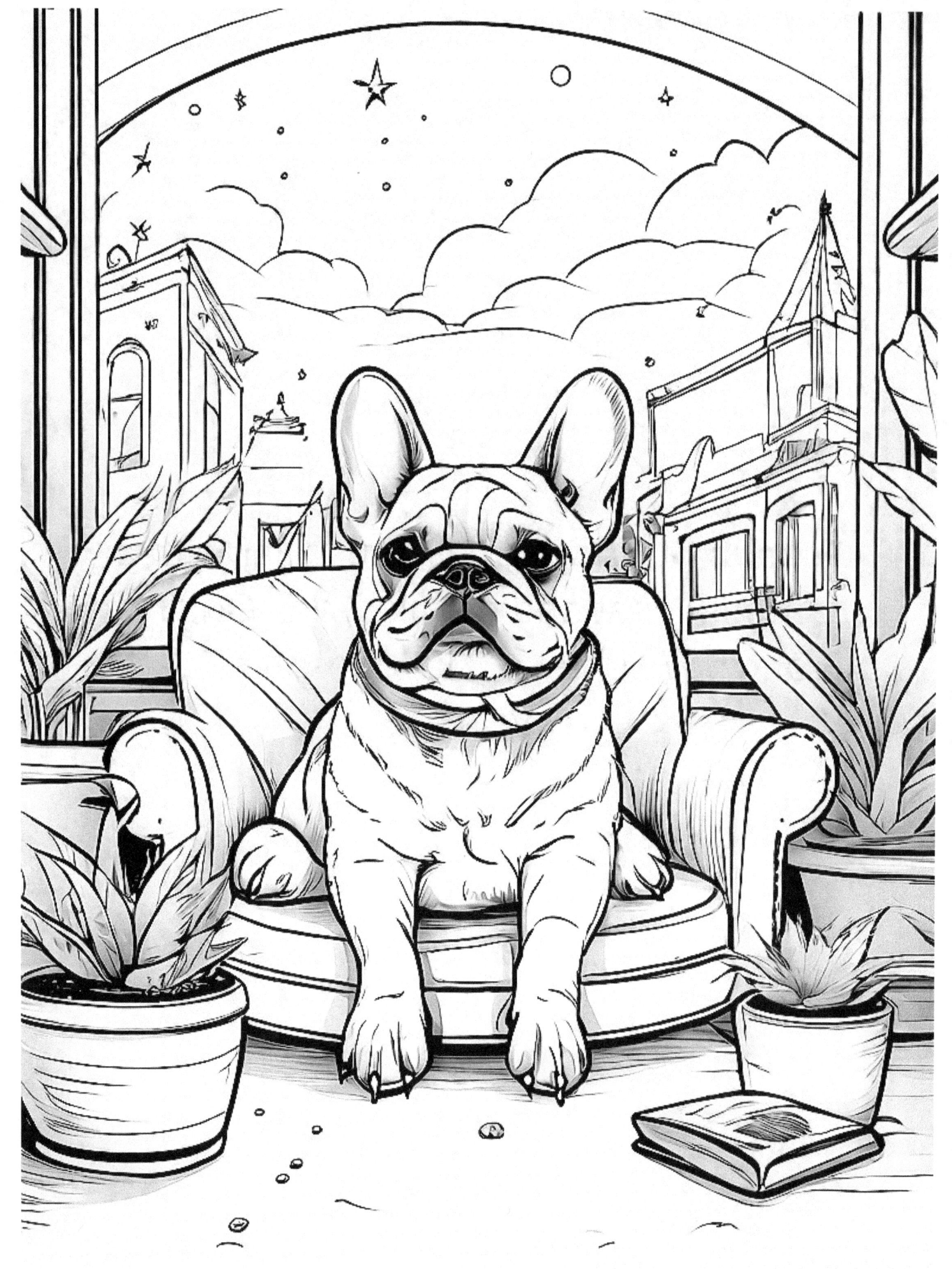

German Spitz: Small to medium-sized, with a fluffy coat and lively personality. Origin: Germany. Weight: 5-20 kg. Lifespan: 13-15 years.

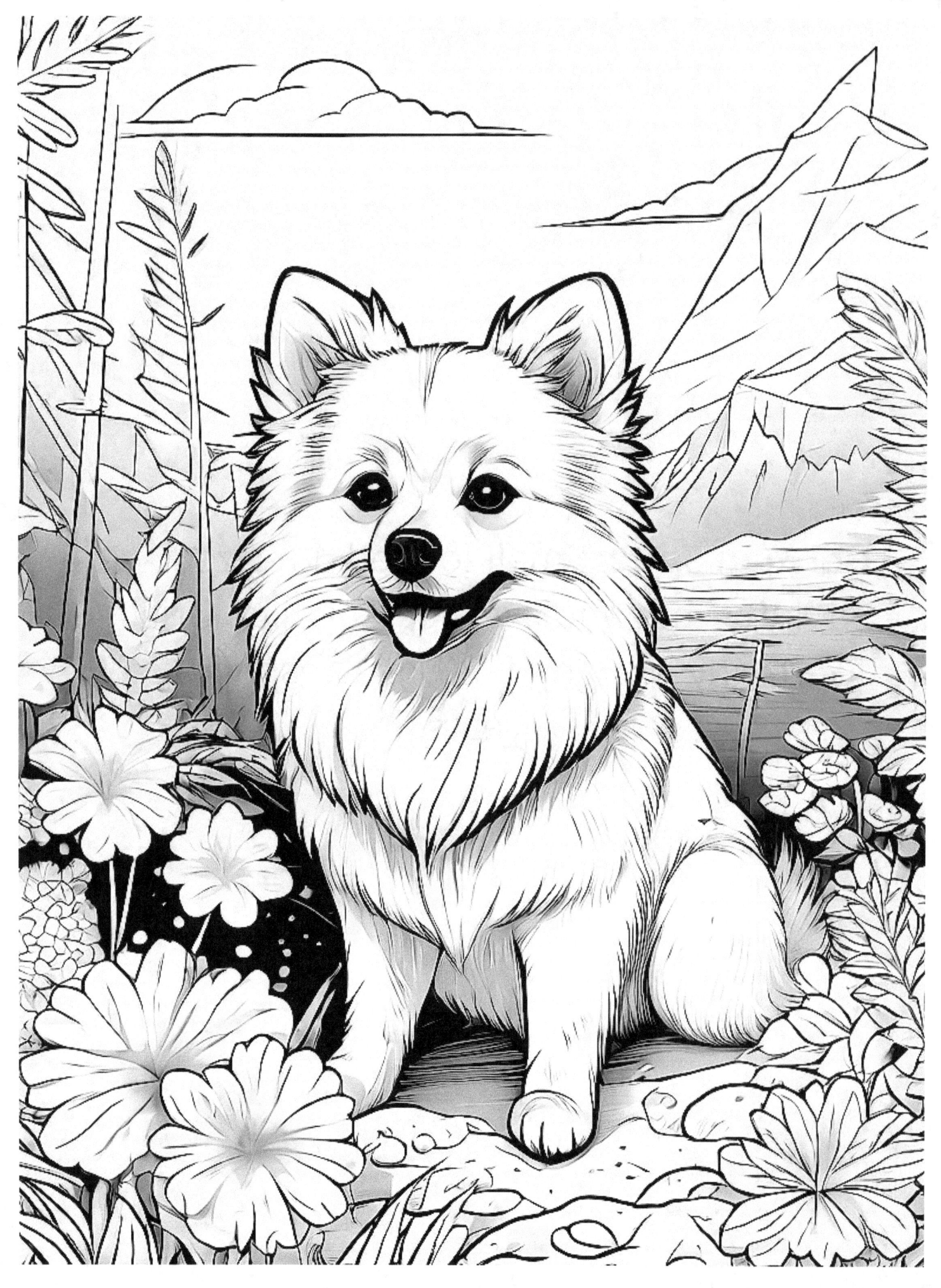

English Cocker Spaniel: Friendly, affectionate, and active. Origin: United Kingdom. Weight: 12-16 kg. Lifespan: 12-15 years.

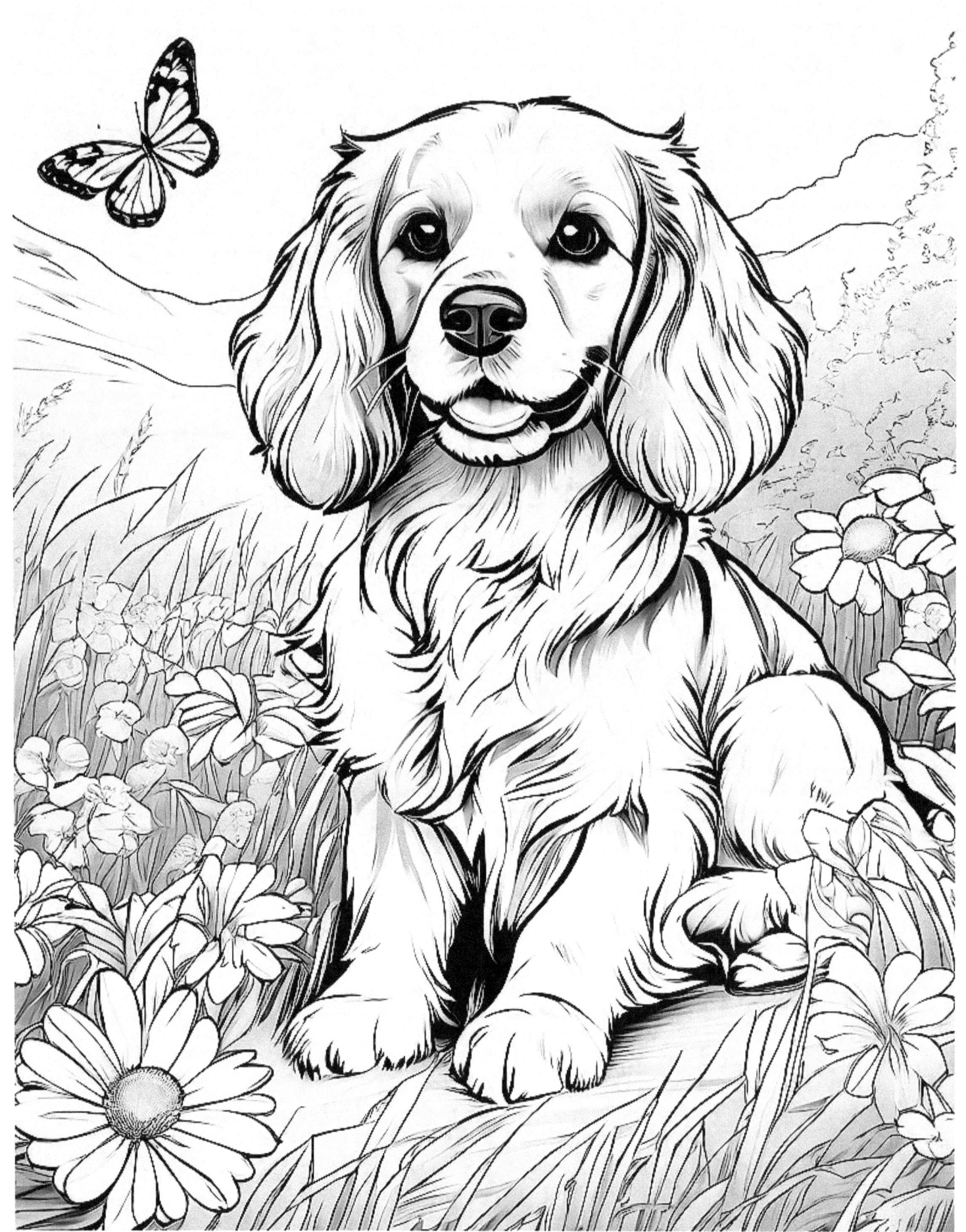

Golden Retriever: Friendly, intelligent, and devoted. Origin: Scotland. Weight: 25-34 kg. Lifespan: 10-12 years.

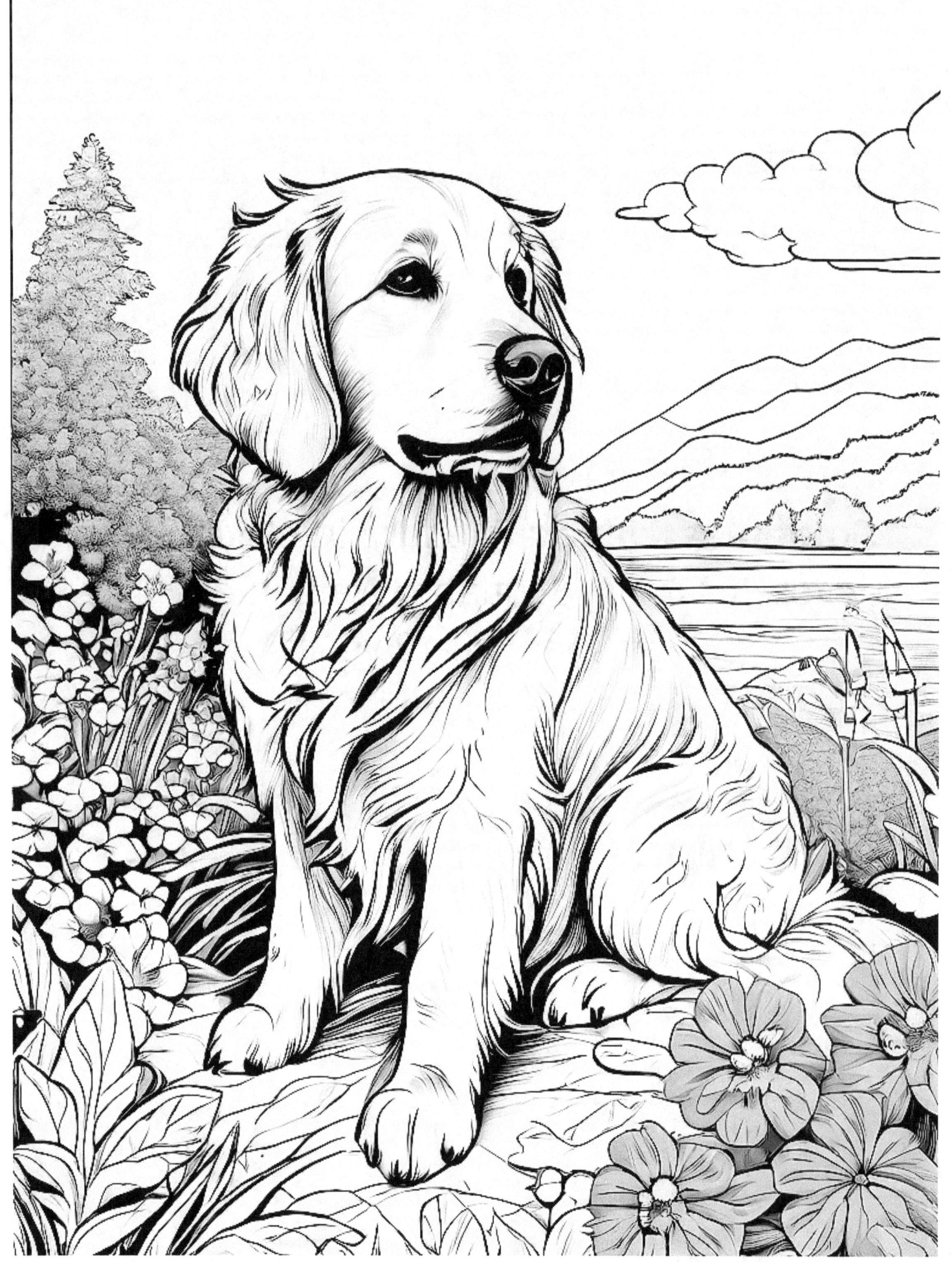

Pekingese: Small, with a long, flowing coat and lion-like appearance. Origin: China. Weight: 3.2-6.4 kg. Lifespan: 12-14 years.

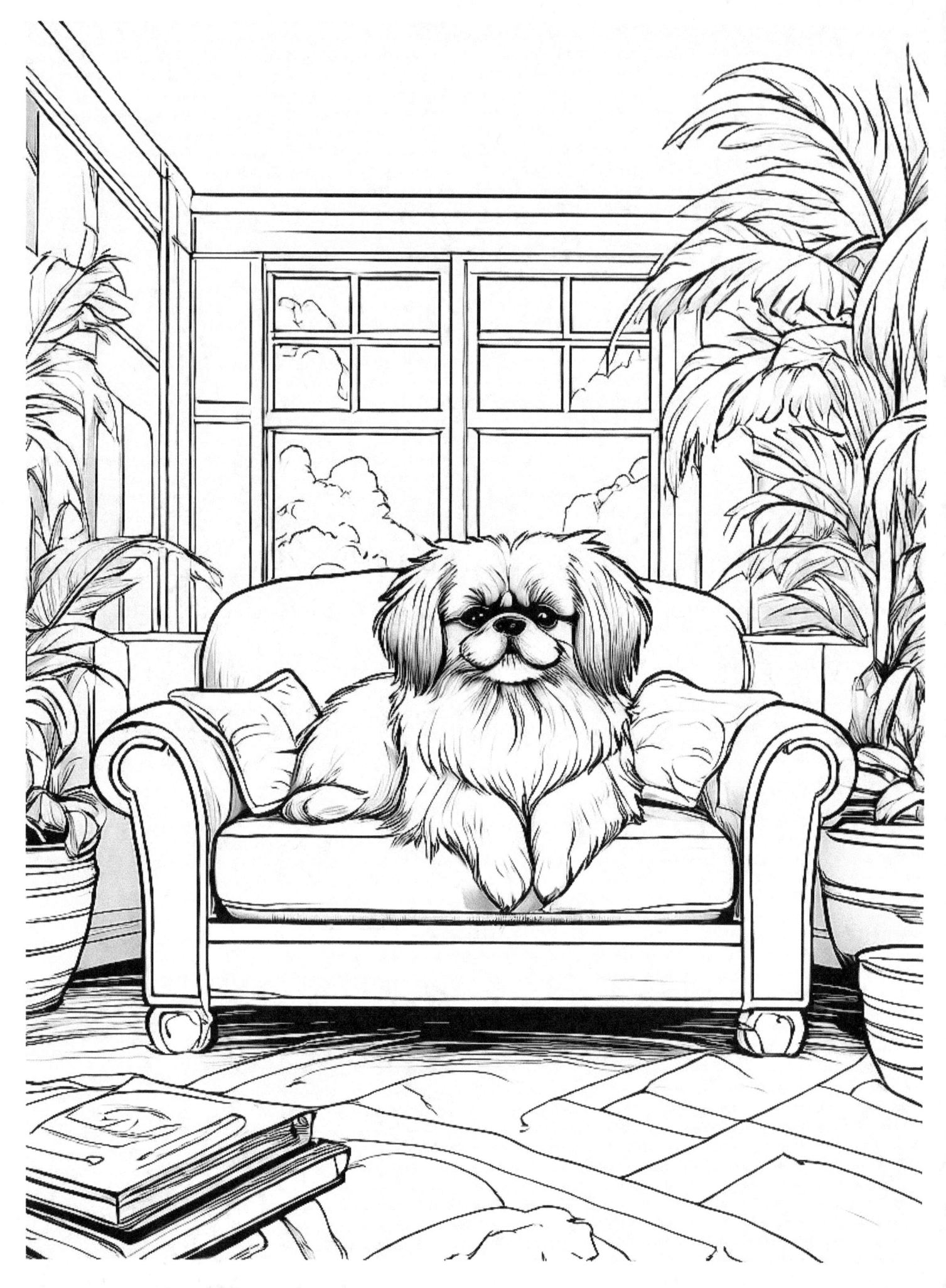

Pharaoh Hound: Sleek and elegant, with a short coat and large, expressive ears. Origin: Malta. Weight: 18-27 kg. Lifespan: 12-14 years.

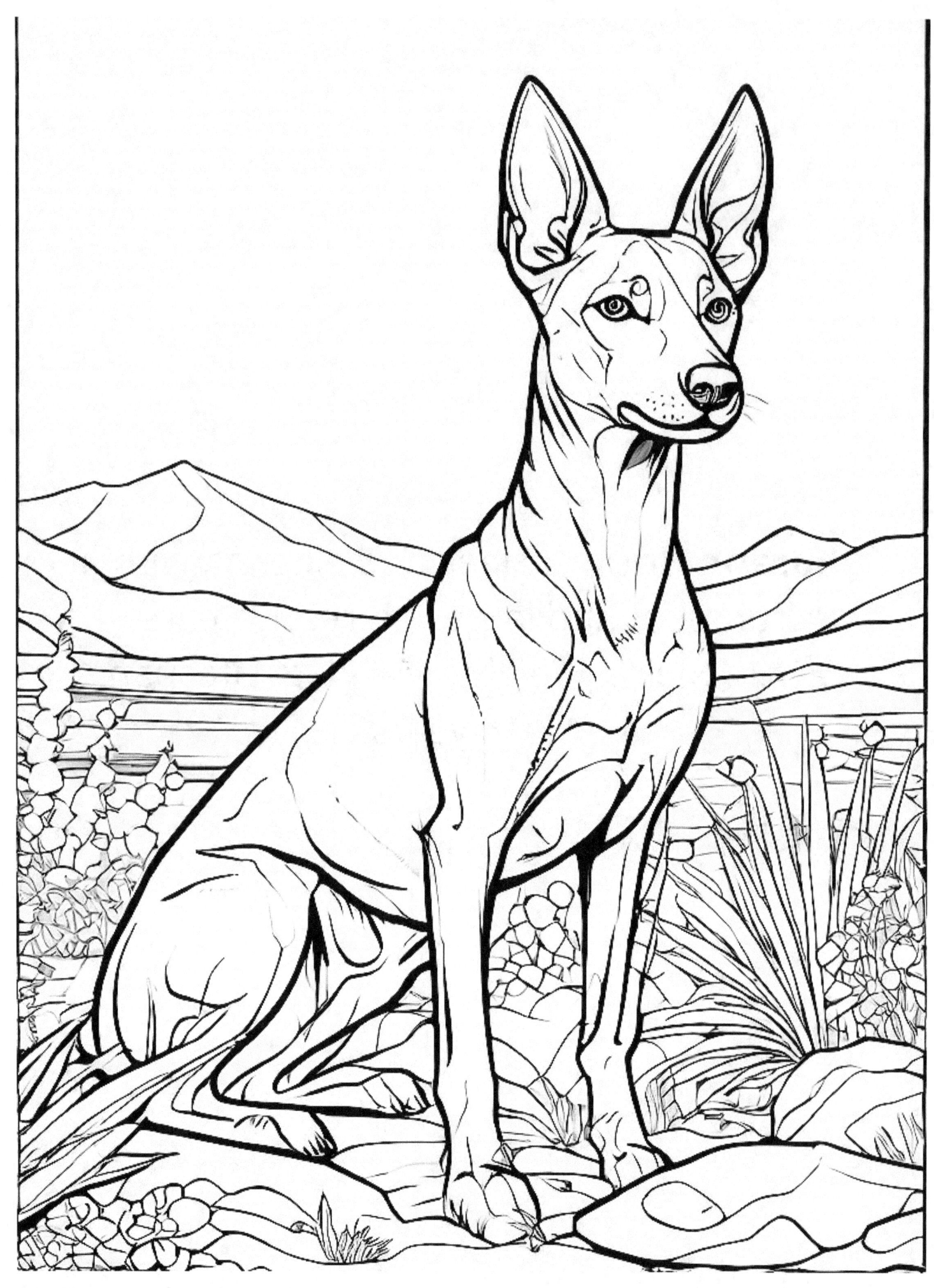

Papillon: Small, with distinctive butterfly-like ears and lively temperament. Origin: France/Belgium. Weight: 3.6-4.5 kg. Lifespan: 12-16 years.

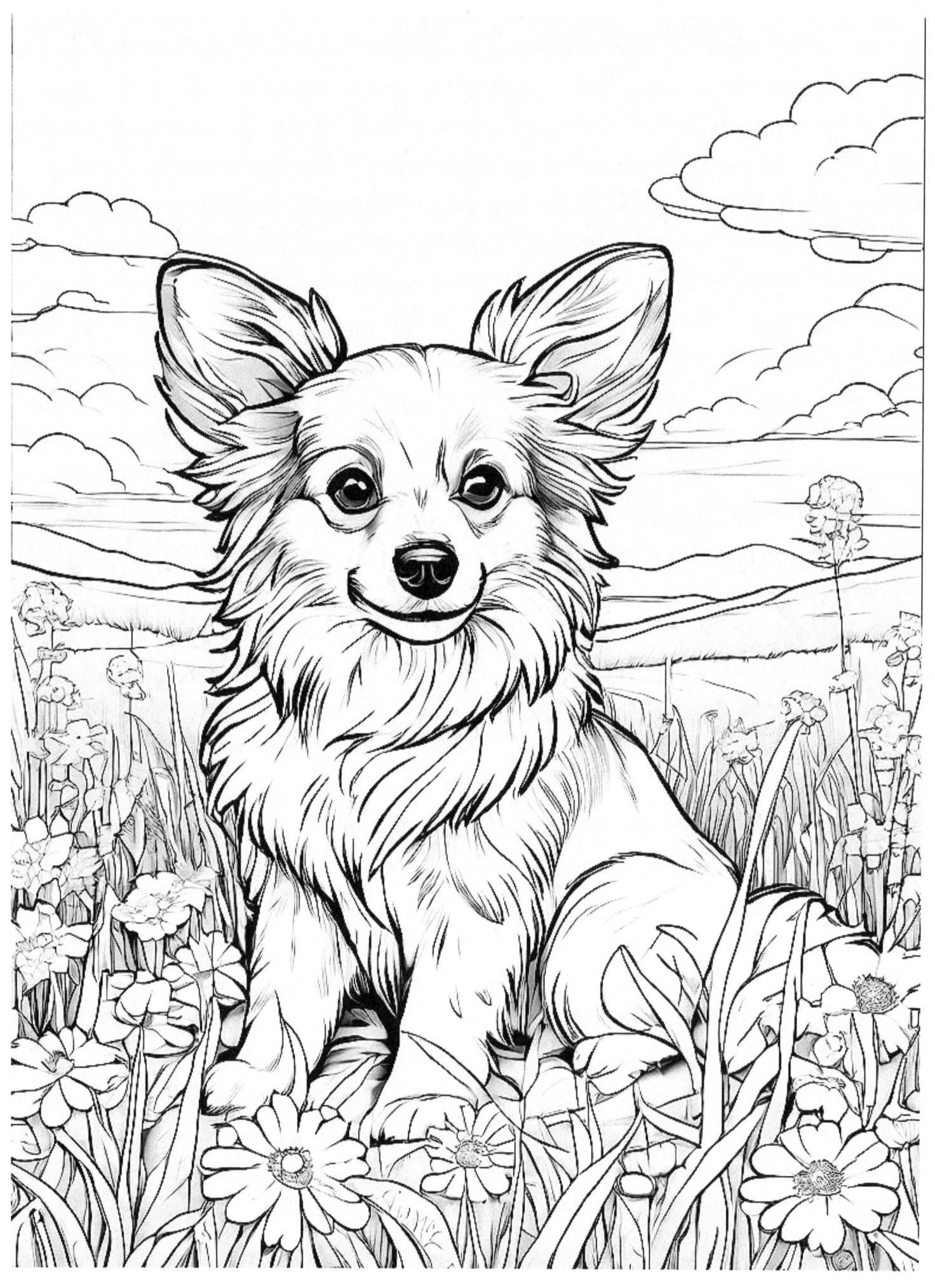

Miniature Pinscher: Small, energetic, and fearless. Origin: Germany. Weight: 3.6-4.5 kg. Lifespan: 12-16 years.

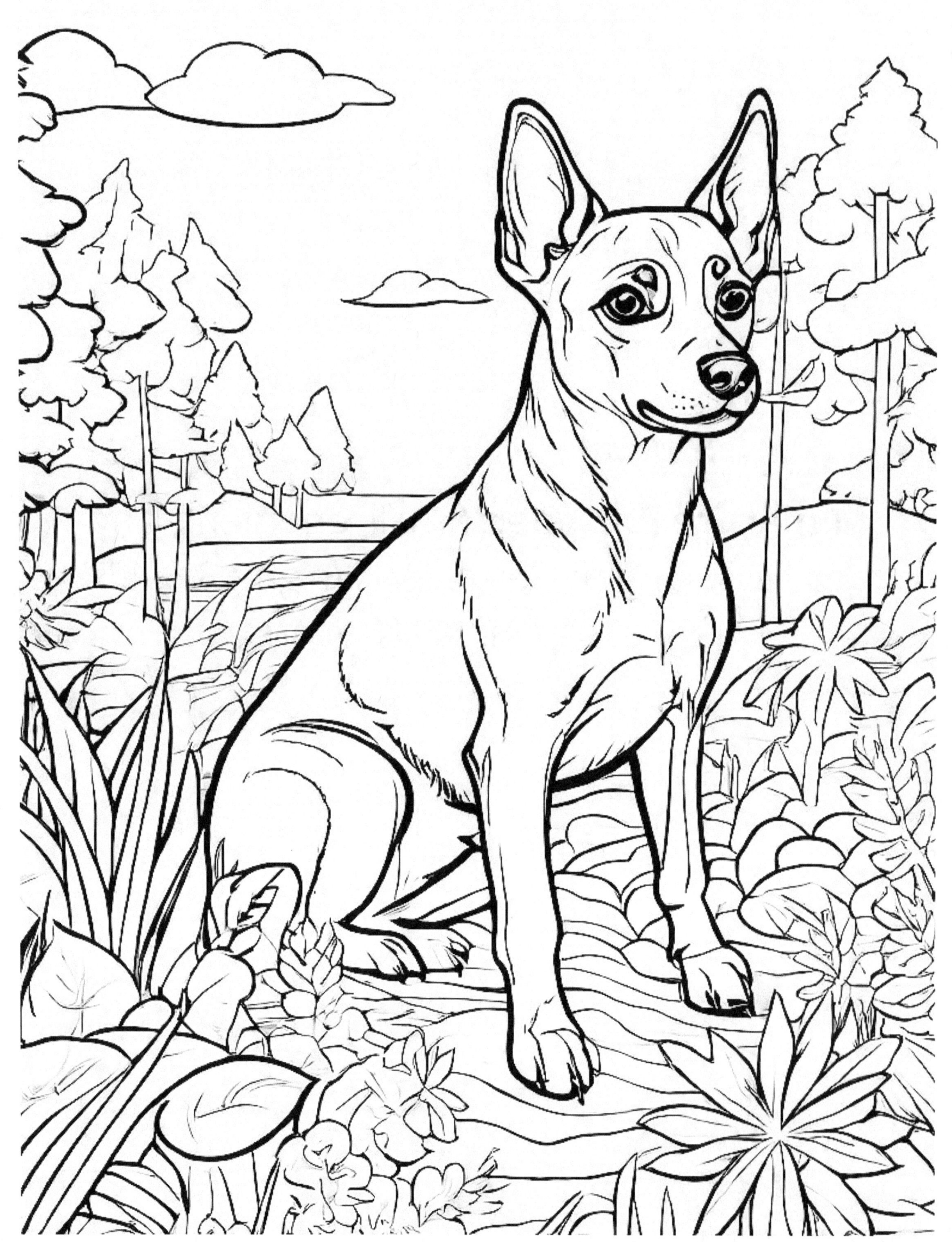

Rottweiler: Strong, loyal, and confident guardian. Origin: Germany. Weight: 35-60 kg. Lifespan: 8-10 years.

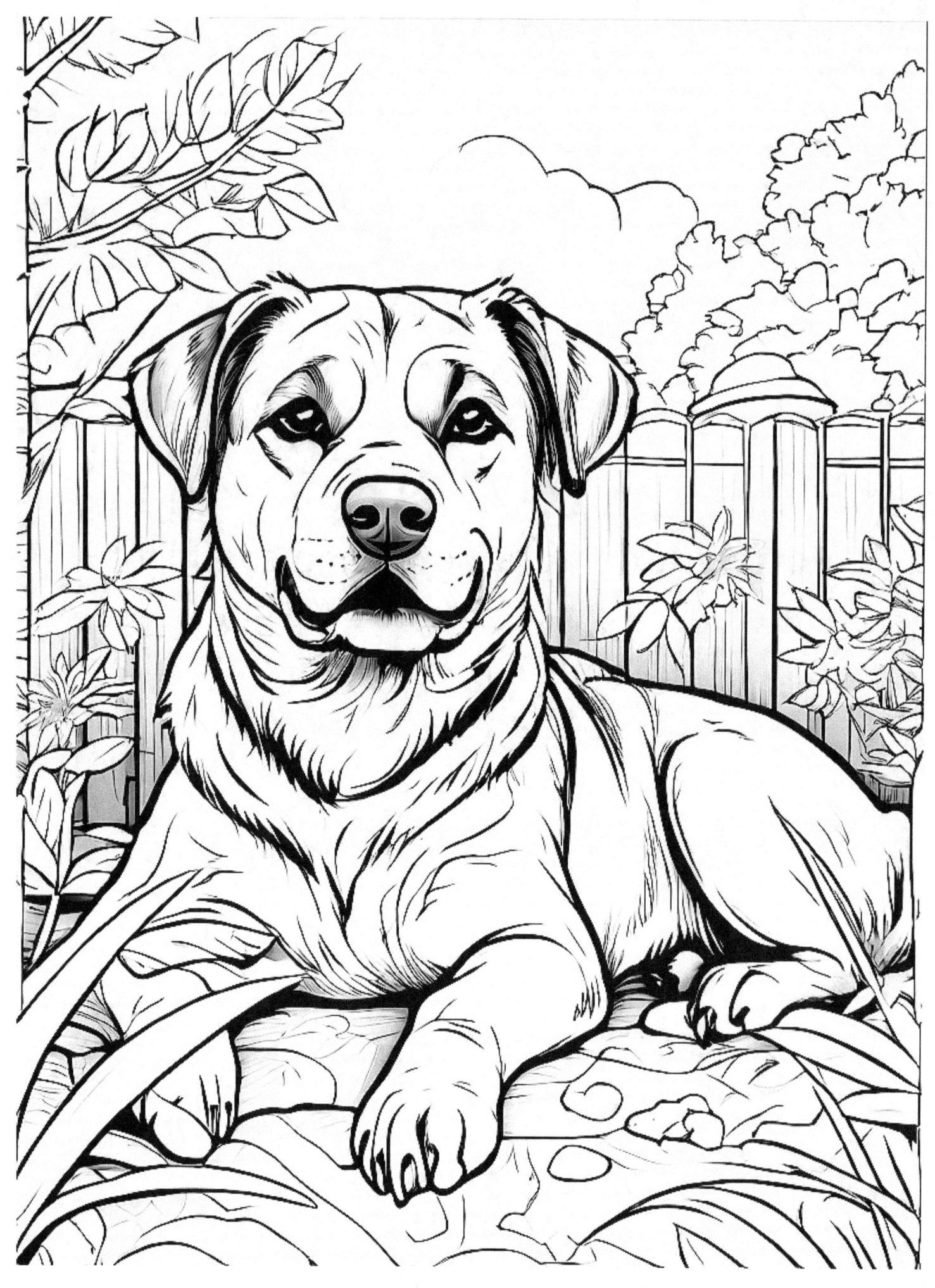

Poodle: Intelligent, versatile, and comes in Standard, Miniature, and Toy sizes. Origin: Germany/France. Weight: 2-32 kg (depending on size). Lifespan: 12-15 years.

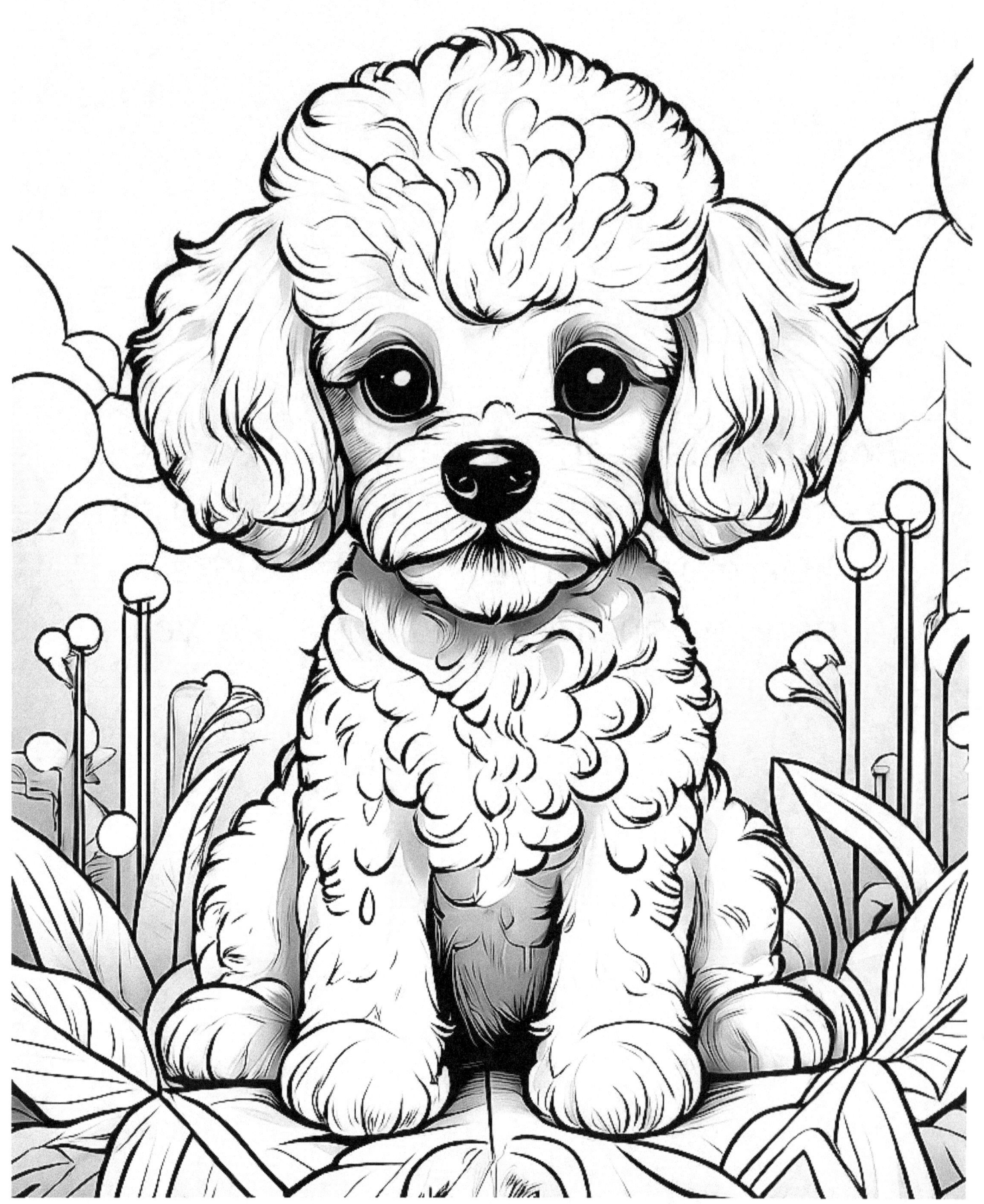

Maltese: Small, with a long, silky white coat and playful personality. Origin: Malta. Weight: 1.4-3.6 kg. Lifespan: 12-15 years.

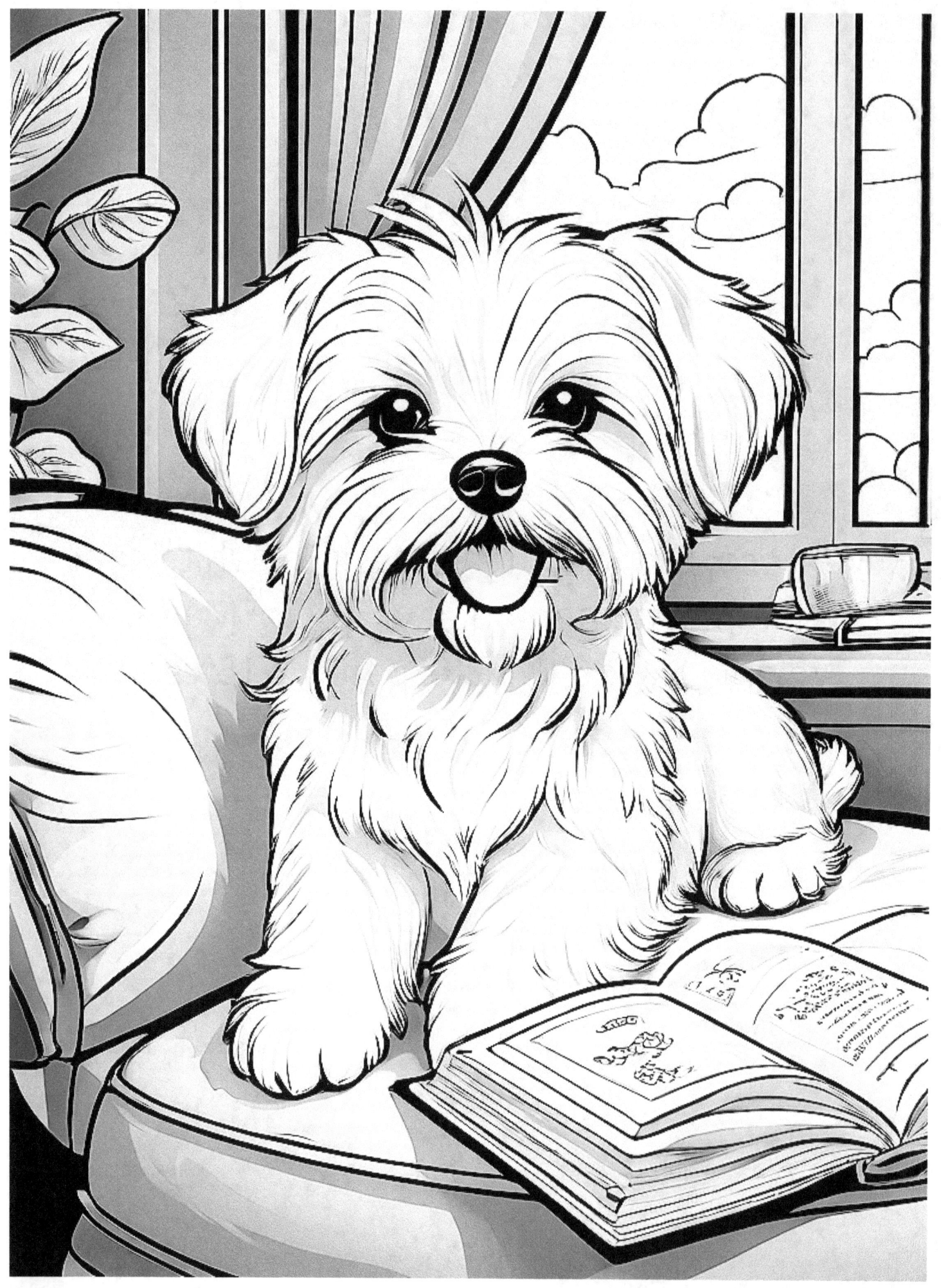

Rhodesian Ridgeback: Known for the distinctive ridge of hair along their back and their athletic build. Origin: Southern Africa. Weight: 29-41 kg. Lifespan: 10-12 years.

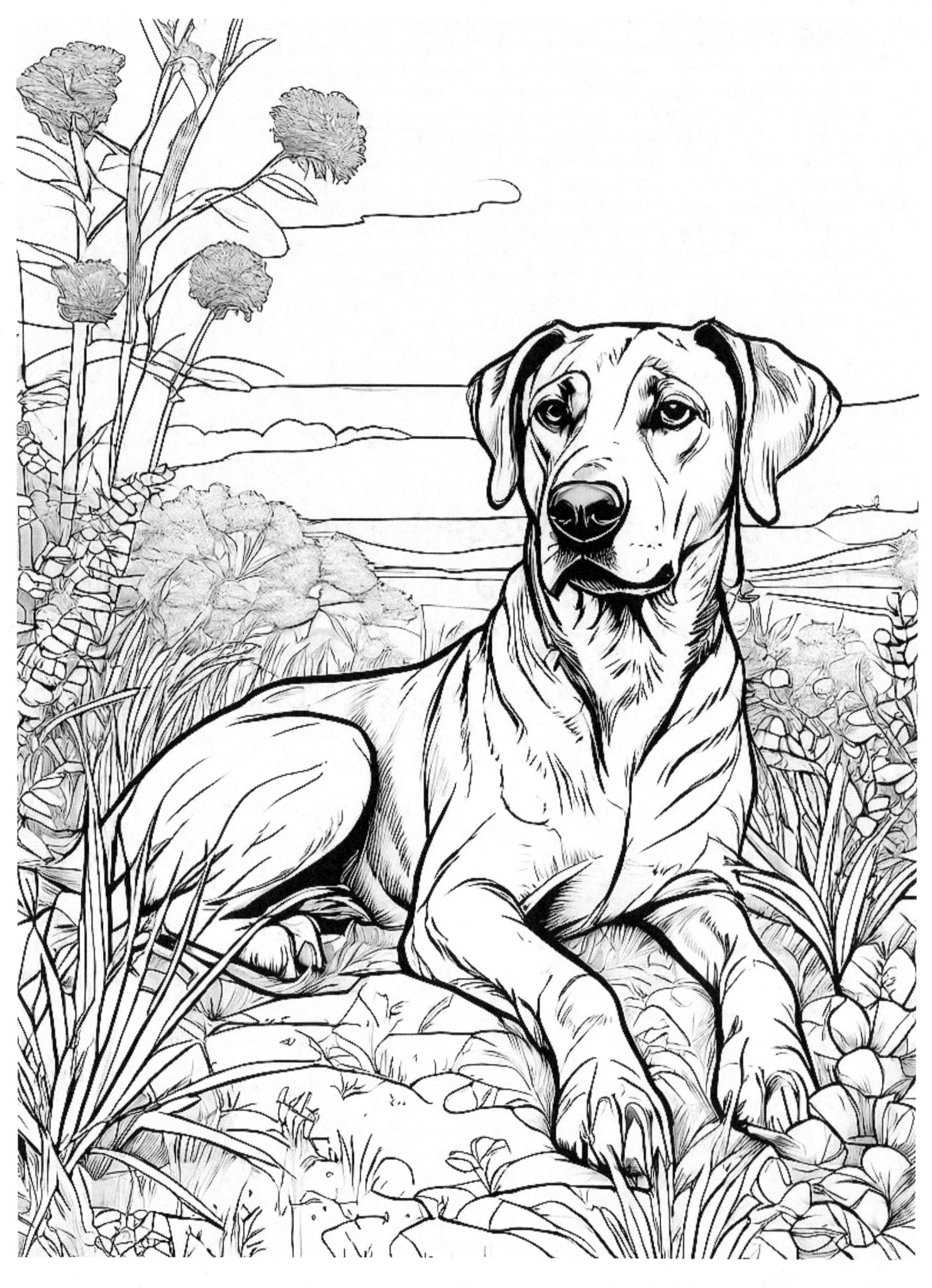

Portuguese Water Dog: Curly-coated and lively, famous for their swimming abilities. Origin: Portugal. Weight: 16-27 kg. Lifespan: 10-14 years.

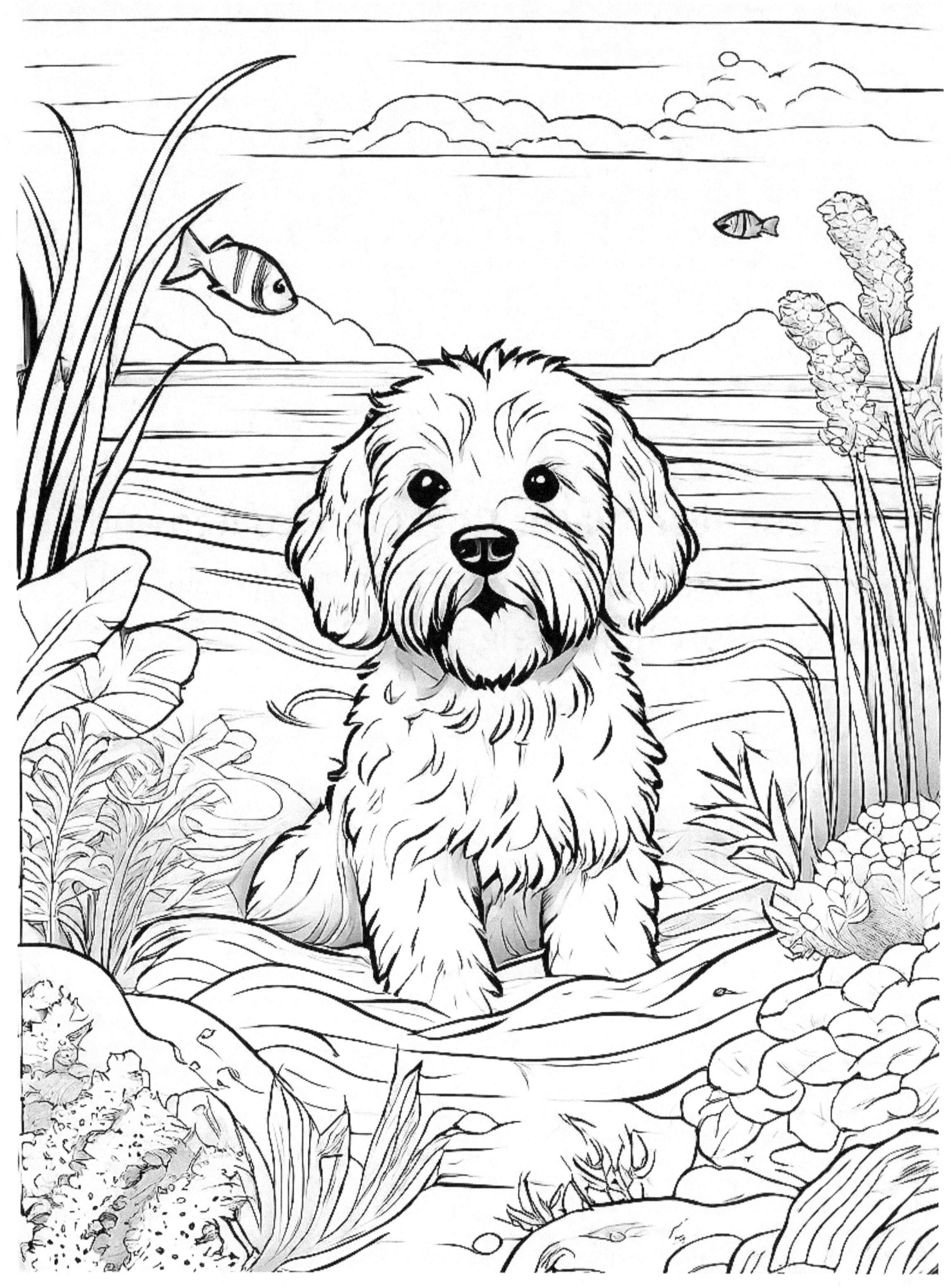

Pomeranian: Small, fluffy, and lively companion. Origin: Germany/Poland. Weight: 1.9-3.5 kg. Lifespan: 12-16 years.

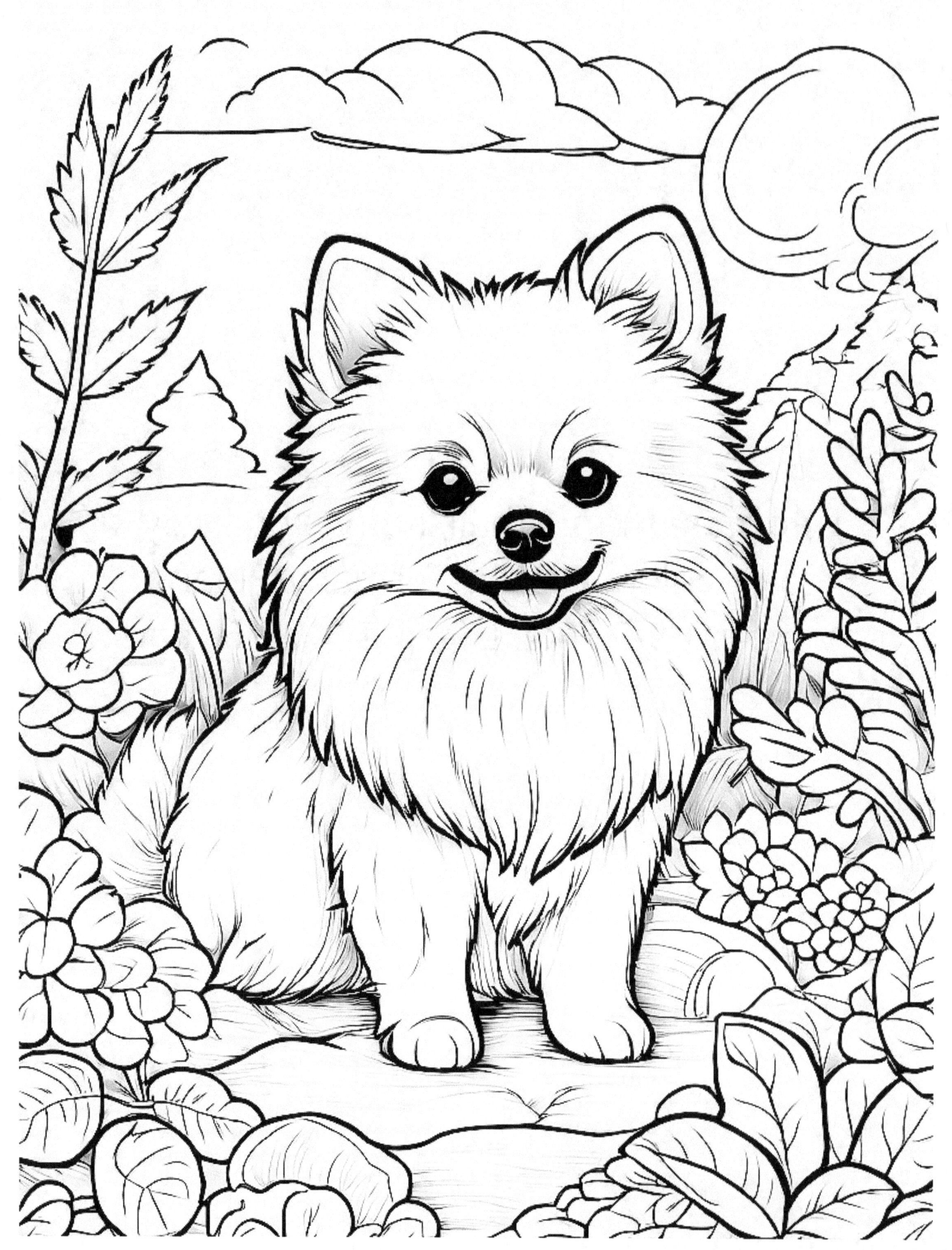

Vizsla: Sleek and elegant with a golden rust coat, known for their affectionate nature. Origin: Hungary. Weight: 20-30 kg. Lifespan: 12-14 years.

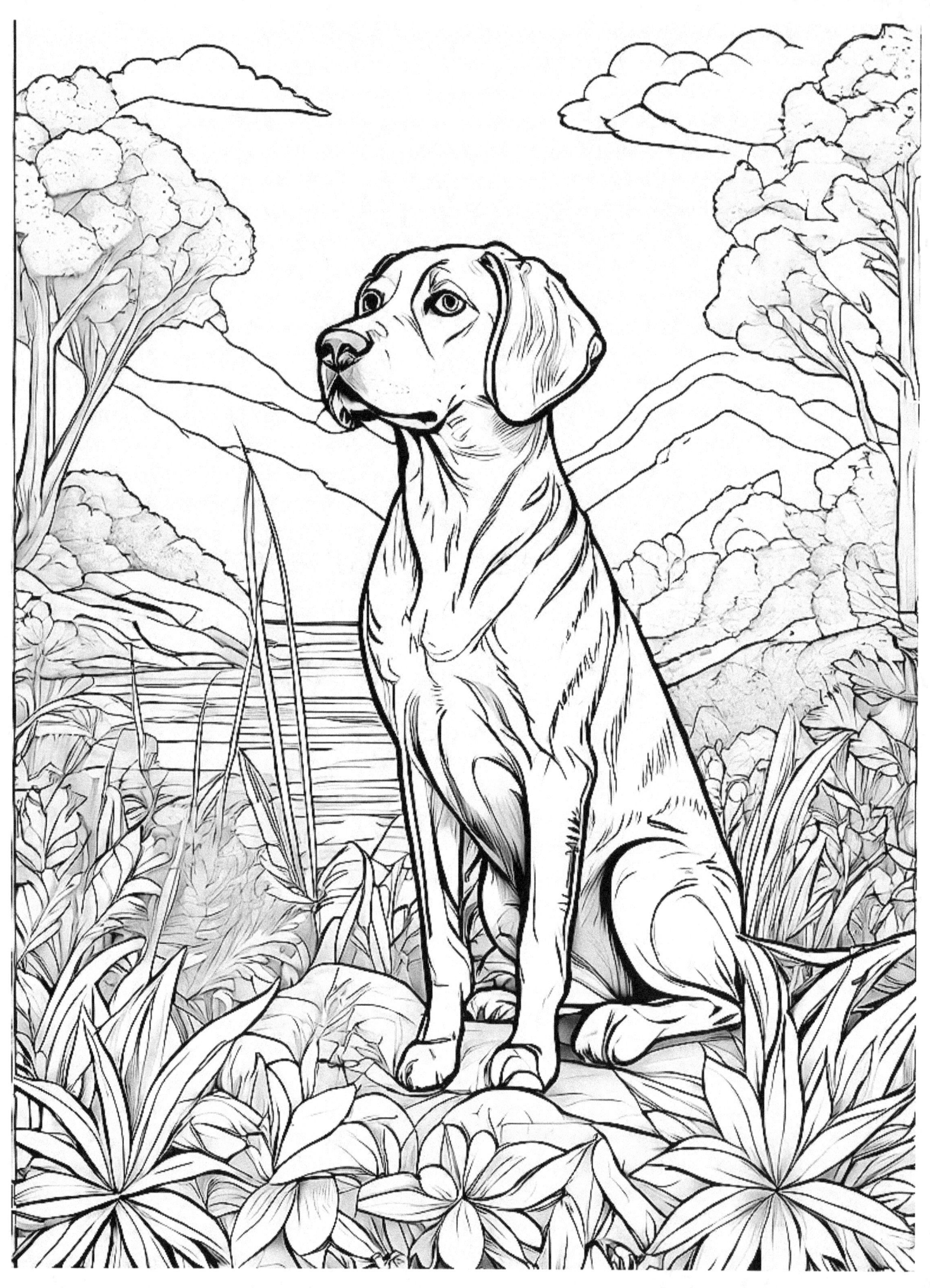

Shetland Sheepdog: Resembling a small Collie, with a long, flowing coat and bright eyes. Origin: Scotland. Weight: 6-12 kg. Lifespan: 12-15 years.

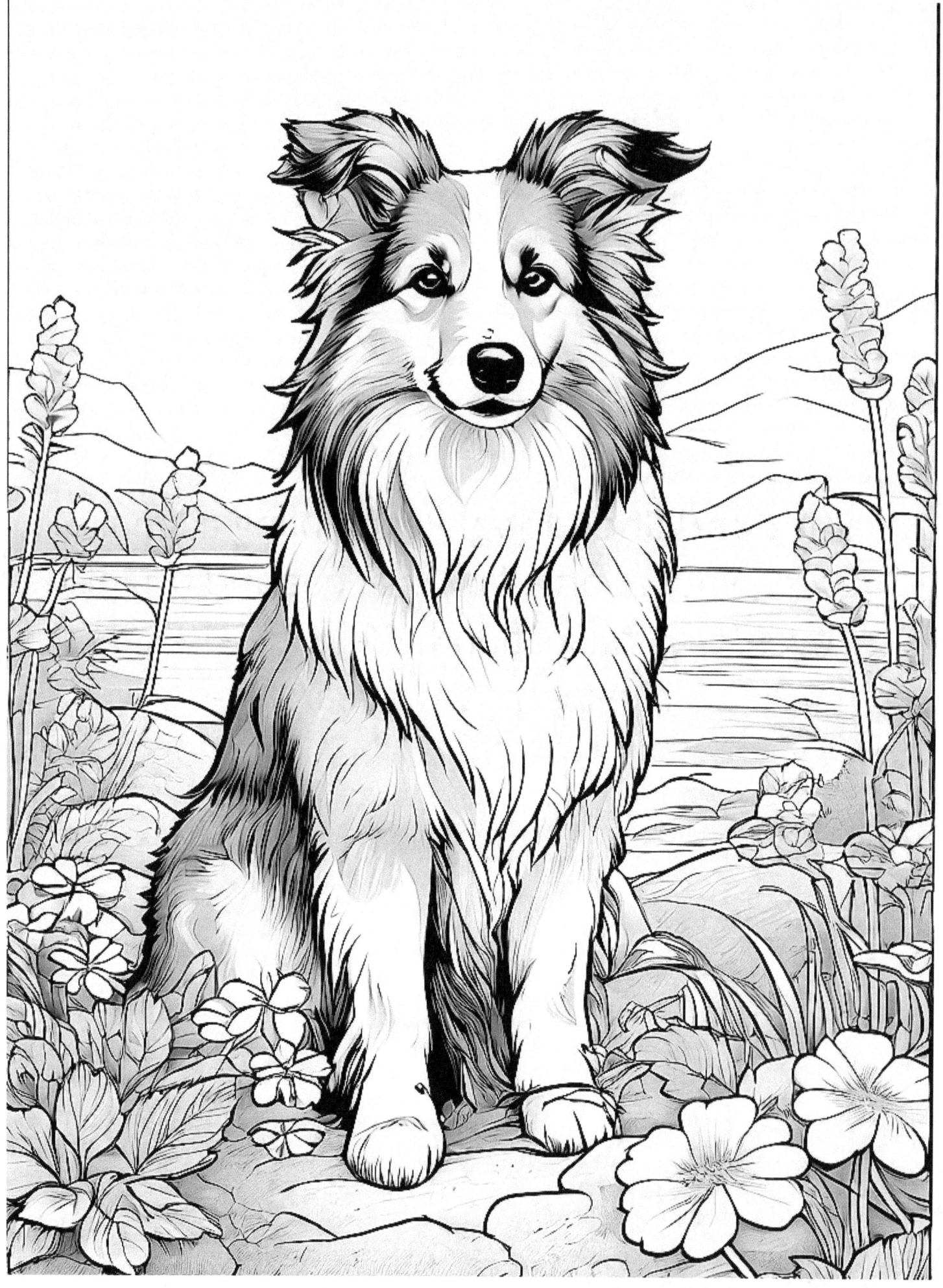

Samoyed: Known for its fluffy white coat and friendly disposition. Origin: Russia. Weight: 20-30 kg. Lifespan: 12-14 years.

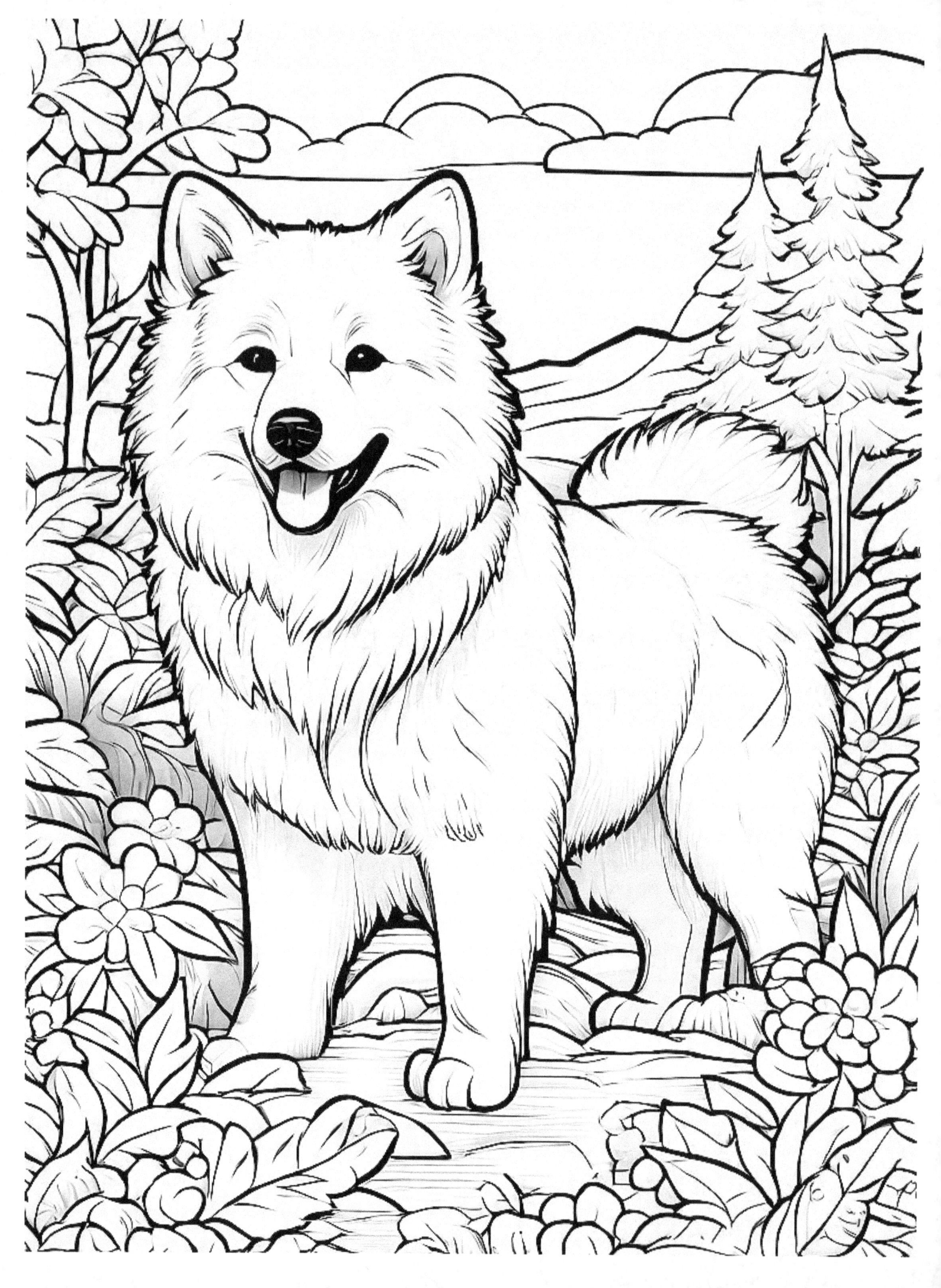

Saluki: Slim, graceful, and one of the oldest dog breeds. Origin: Middle East. Weight: 18-27 kg. Lifespan: 12-14 years.

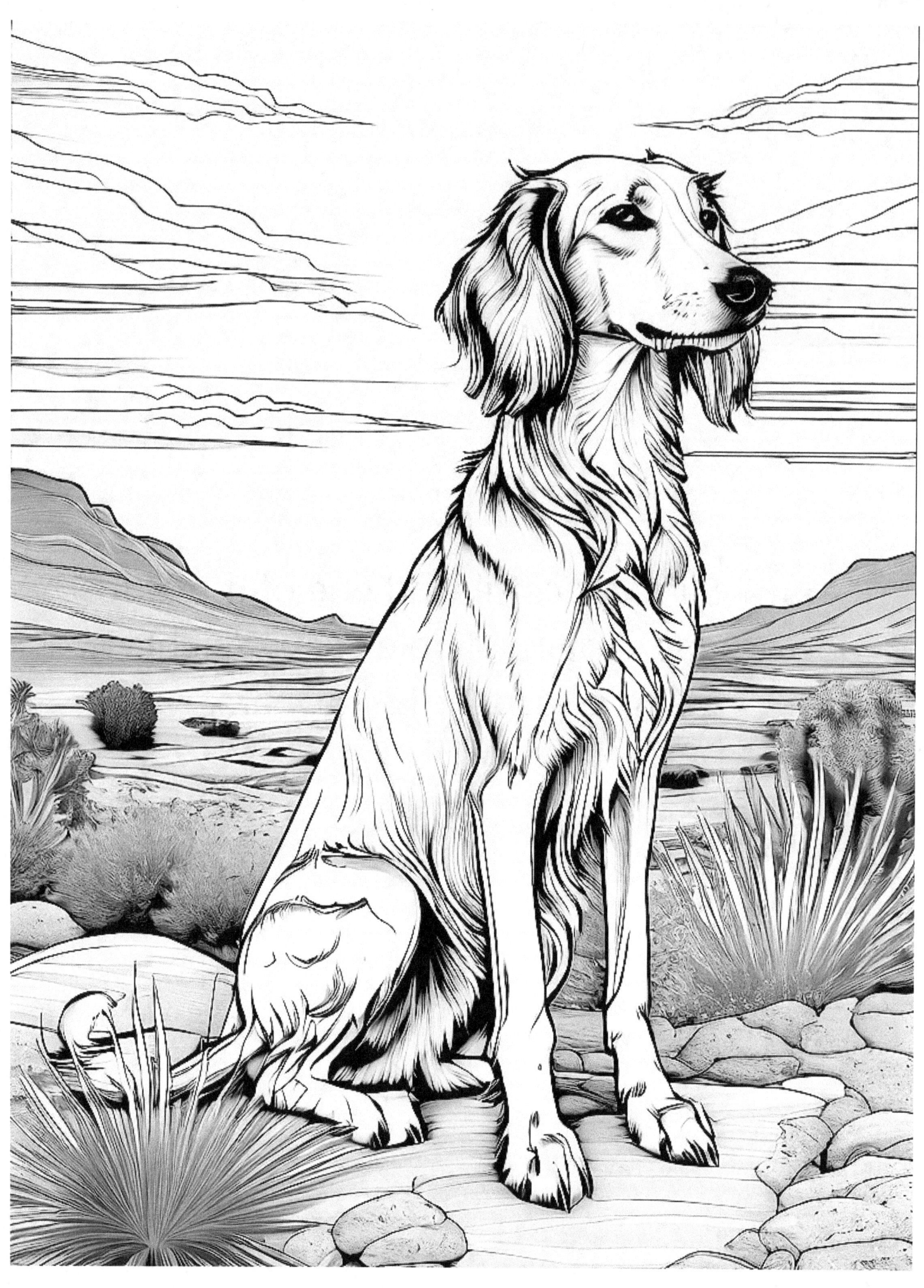

Shih Tzu: Toy breed with a long, flowing double coat. Origin: China. Weight: 4-7 kg. Lifespan: 10-16 years.

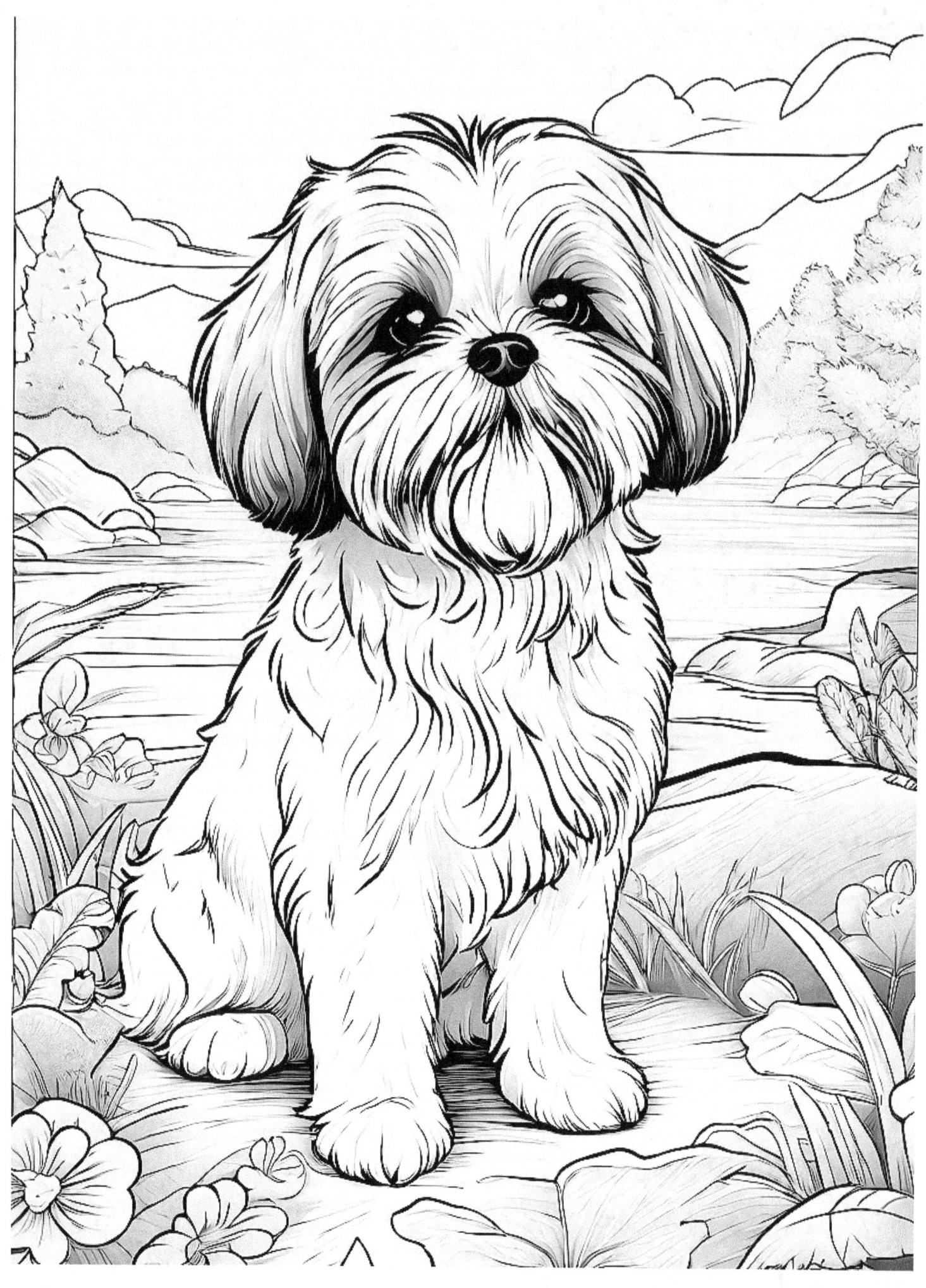

The Brazilian Mastiff, or Fila Brasileiro, is a large, powerful breed from Brazil, known for its loyalty and protective nature.

Origin: Brazil
Weight: 50-82 kg
Lifespan: 9-11 years

Fila Brasileiros are excellent guard dogs and loyal companions, needing experienced handling and early socialization. They are gentle with their family despite their imposing look.

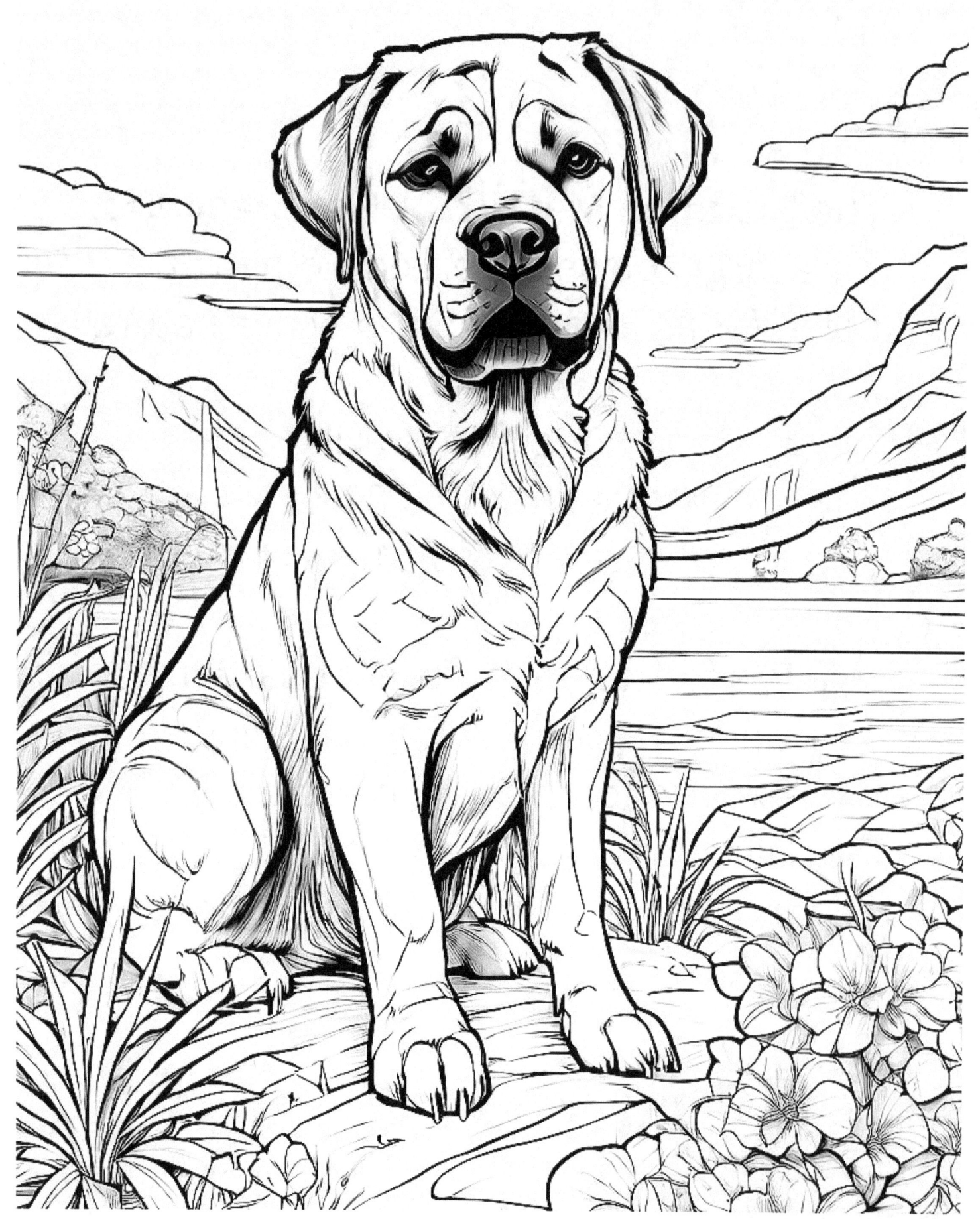

Shiba Inu: Small, agile, and fox-like with a charming expression. Origin: Japan. Weight: 8-10 kg. Lifespan: 12-15 years.

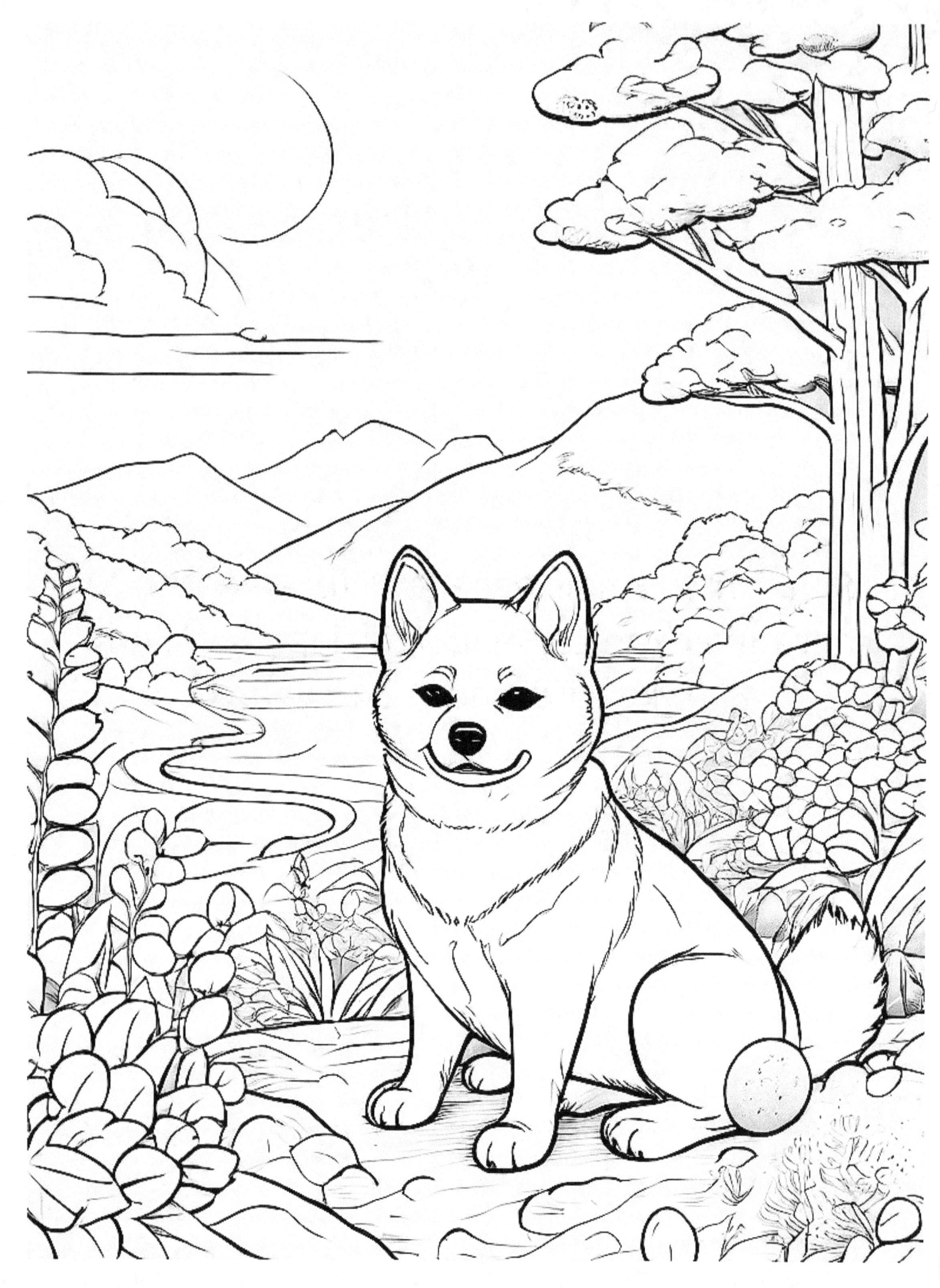

Weimaraner: Known for its sleek silver-gray coat and athletic build. Origin: Germany. Weight: 25-40 kg. Lifespan: 10-13 years.

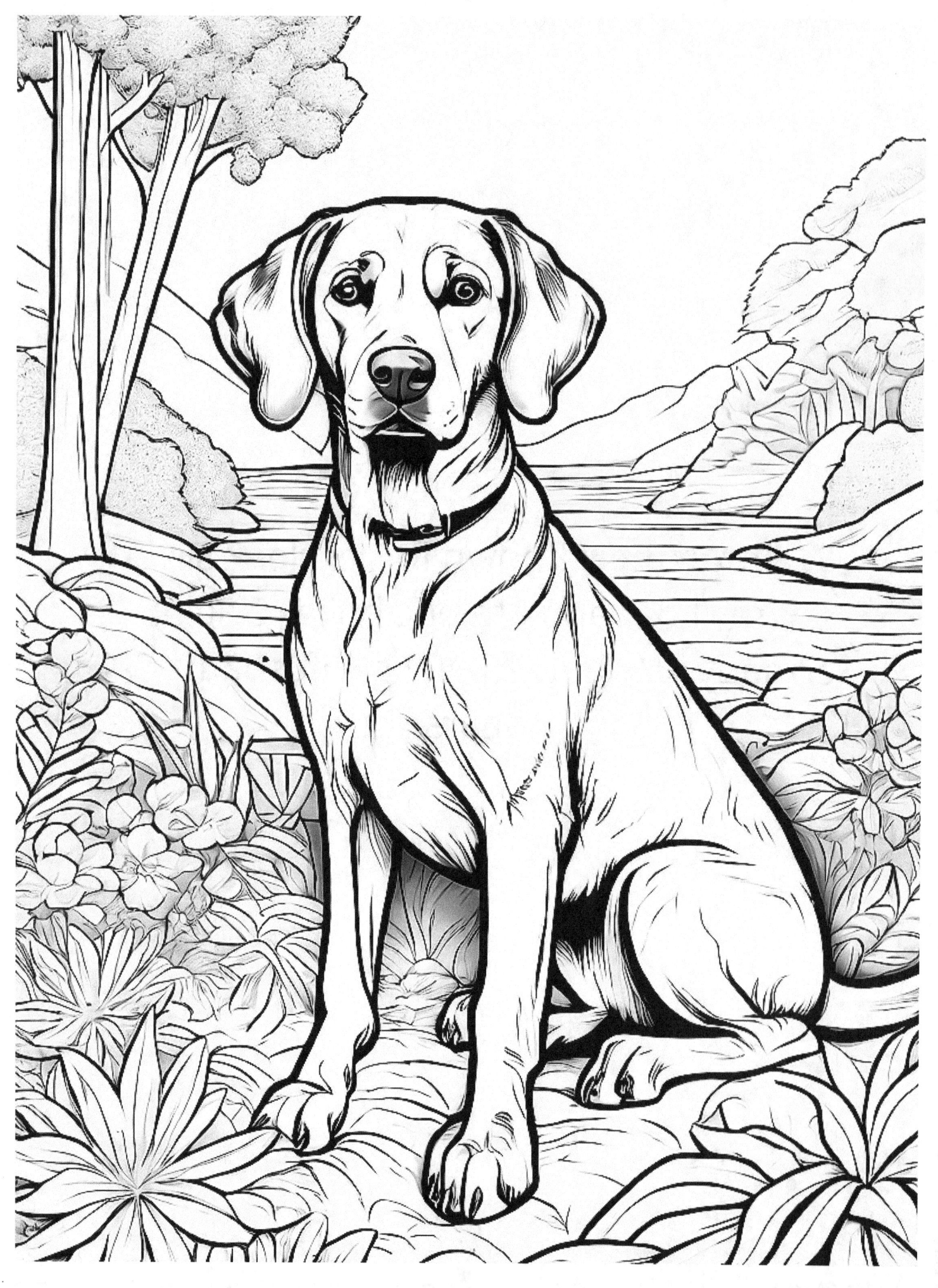

Whippet: Slim, athletic, and known for its speed. Origin: United Kingdom. Weight: 9-20 kg. Lifespan: 12-15 years.

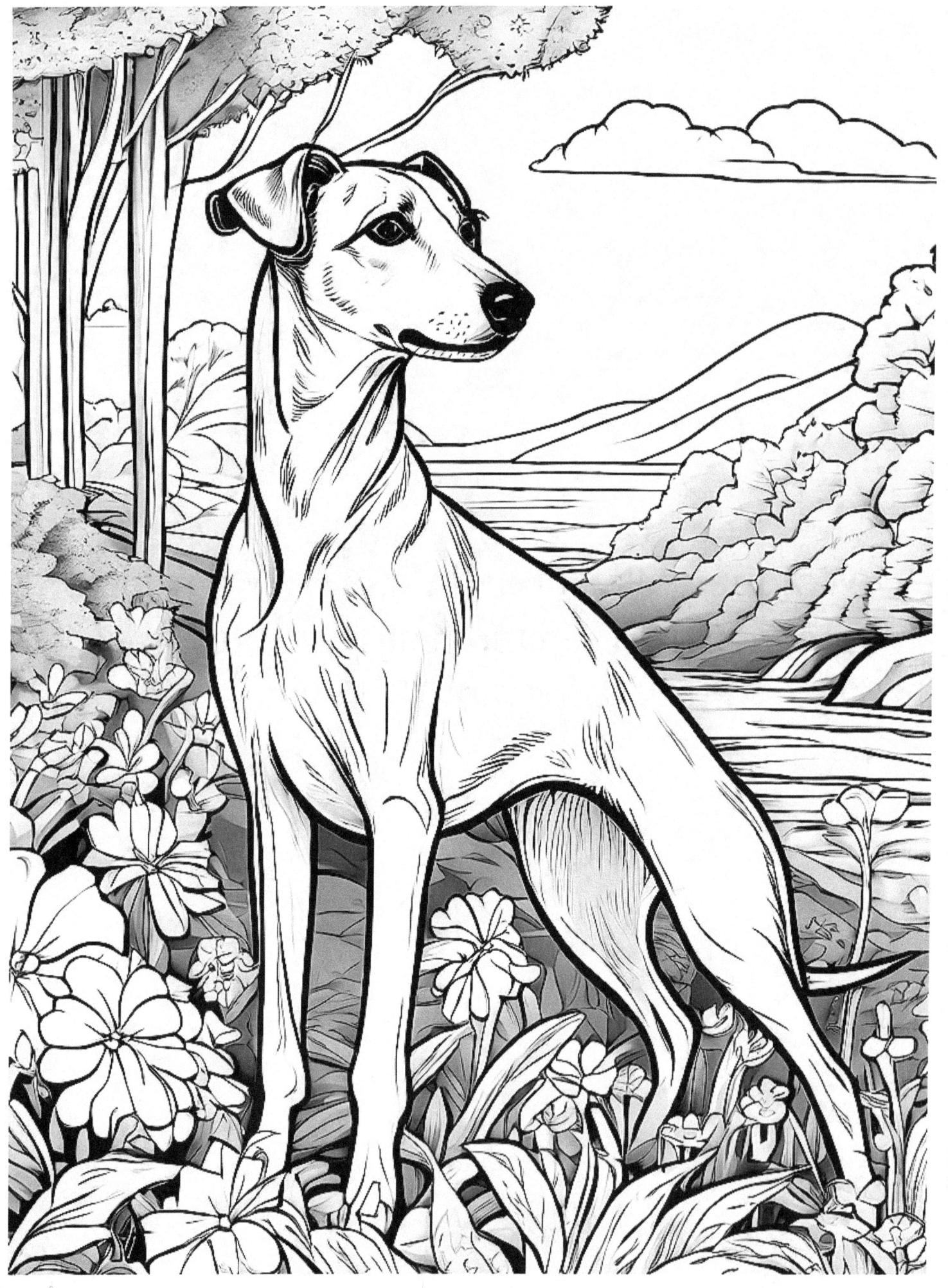

The Pitbull, or American Pit Bull Terrier, is a muscular breed from the United States.

Origin: United States
Weight: 14-30 kg
Lifespan: 12-16 years

Pitbulls are strong, agile, and friendly, needing regular exercise and socialization.

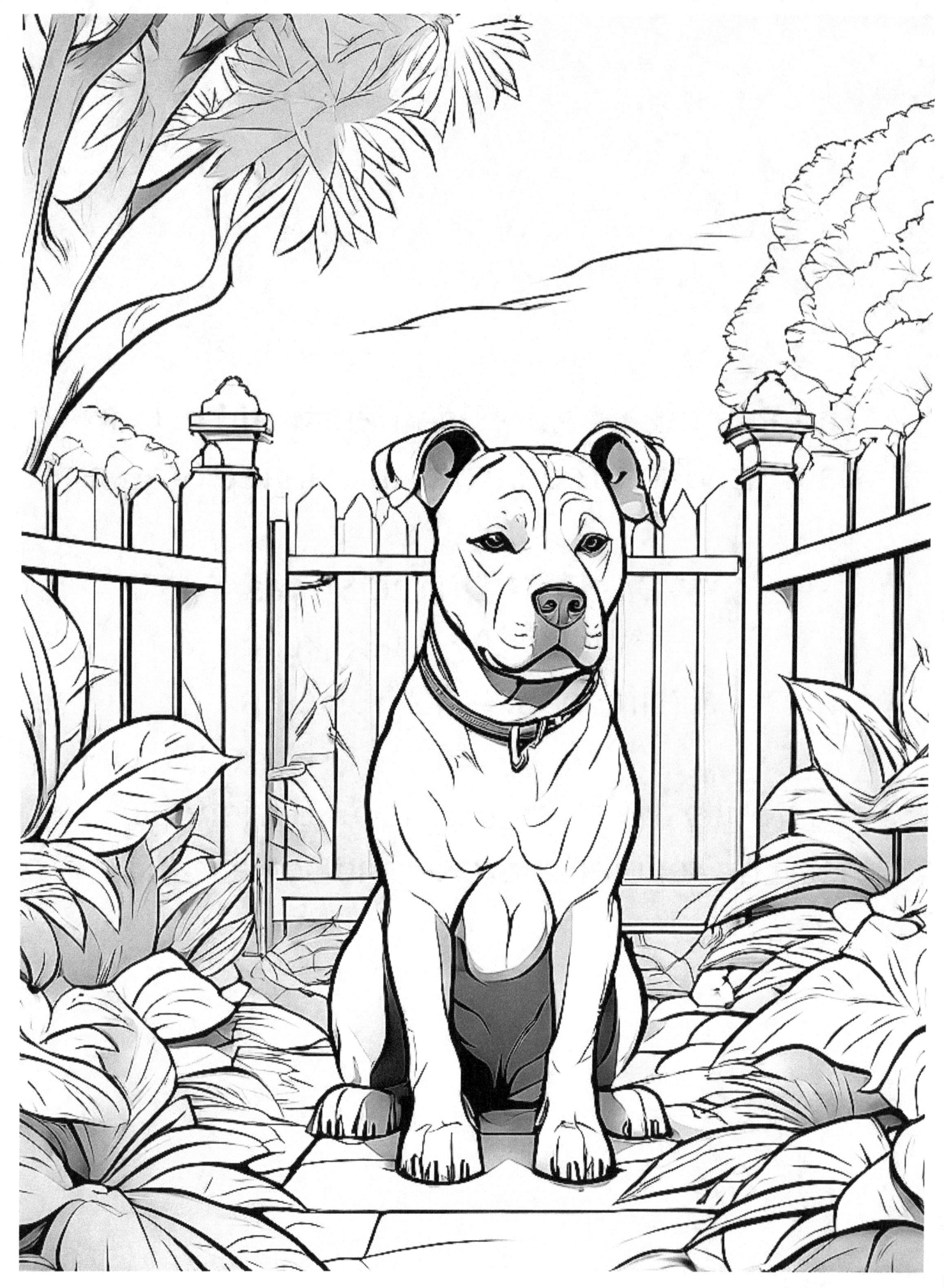

www.ingramcontent.com/pod-product-compliance
Lightning Source LLC
Chambersburg PA
CBHW082211220526
45470CB00010B/3119